The European Self-Image
in the Midst of Change

A New History of the Origin of Our Core Values

Harald Haarmann & LaBGC

Index of contents

1

Illustrations
"No more powerlessness – doing something for the world doesn't always mean signing 15 petitions, organizing three vigils, or chaining yourself to a tree."

(Ronja von Rönne, DIE ZEIT, 2 October 2018)

Introduction: Orientation and Attitude

In our world and its more or less democratic institutions, we are confronted with issues caused by populism, political fanaticism and extremism, intolerance, technocracy, bureaucracy and the ideologization of interpersonal concerns. And on top of the current warlike conflicts in the world, there is now another war in Europe. Political disturbances of a special kind challenge us, such as the aggressive xenophobia as the xenophobic poverty of those who are unwilling to cooperate and seek the humanitarian options of the global refugee misery, turning a blind eye to the migratory movements and their triggers. The political pressure on the democratic order is growing, and this puts us in a precarious position: the liberal Europe is under siege and runs the risk of undermining its fundamental values and of stenciling their meaning. Despite all verbal efforts to uphold fundamental values and the maintenance of the democratic order, its contents are in danger of falling by the wayside.

The general feeling of insecurity is reinforced by the political exchange of blows on the world stage, and we are catapulted into an uncontrollable dimension via the imponderability of the flow of information directed through the mass media. In the past, the maxim of a commitment to the truth was taken into account. This was linked to the work ethic of journalists. That was consensus. It seems that the love of truth is more and more overshadowed by the shadow of the information manipulation driven by particular interests. At the same time, the work of journalists all over the world is under threat and has never been more dangerous. The truth content of the information mediation is relativized in the field of tension between the fake news

5

and the total truth decay. The essence of finding truth seems to be evaporating.

Are we moving in a direction where the basic values are no longer needed in the assumption that the problems of our time have no solution? Will an epoch come when more and more people tend to declare basic values as old-fashioned ballast? And did the conclusion mean that the basic values only become nostalgic set pieces stated in our history books? Will the spectrum of political order principles shift in favor of a dictatorial order of different colors? Unfortunately, nowadays, such questions can no longer be ruled out without further ado.

There is widespread concern that nothing can be done about the emptying of meaning in society, and with the feeling of powerlessness, there is a growing concern that the decline of civilization cannot be stopped. "Fainting is like most sensations: it is a feeling, and feelings are very self-confident. Indeed, they are much more self-confident than reason" (von Rönne 2018).

The accumulation of issues is the main characteristic of the current phase in which we experience history: the pandemic, the war in Ukraine and all the associated pan-European and global effects make unmistakably clear that we live in a threshold epoch. What we need is solidarity – with the necessary safety margin – and the unprejudiced public discussion of different attitudes. This applies once again to the handling of the war in Ukraine. We are in the upheaval of an epoch which is coming to an end and are looking hard and tense at the new epoch which is not yet opening up to us. There were many upheavals, the last major upheaval was the change from the 19th to the 20th century. The slavist and linguist Uwe Hinrichs states the following:

"Many elements which marked the change from the 19th to the 20th century can still be found today: exhaustion, insecurity, utopias, premonitions, visions, the mood of the end times. When things go well, the loss of orientation eventually turns into a radical change, into the vision of a new horizon on which things reappear in a new shape, in a like from the no-man's land of the turn of the times" (Hinrichs 2018: 1).

It would be fatal if we allowed our basic values to weaken so much in the wake of the pandemic and in the search for solutions to end the war in Ukraine that only fragments remained. The basic values are also indispensable in the "new" epoch. Like the term democracy, they are susceptible to demagogic, populist, ideological and extremist attacks of all kinds. However, this does not reduce their essential importance. On the contrary, the basic values are demanding, both from the point of view of their content and from the point of view of their effect, once they are able to exploit the room for maneuver they deserve within a political order. The basic values need to be anchored in our consciousness. If the awareness of their importance were weakened, this would weaken the state administration itself. This would result in a loss of flexibility and in the beginning of an encrustation. The basic values would be distorted or even emptied of their meaning.

The term "democracy" is often used again for good reasons, and even dictators engage in verbal feats of strength about democratic order, rulers who present themselves as democrats since they do not ostentatiously appear as autocrats. The concept "democracy" has already been bent in any direction. According to the North Korean interpretation, even North Korea is a state having a democratic order.

In fact, in North Korea all citizens are granted the freedom to cheer on the "father of the country". If democracy is just invoked in a penetrating way without any historical foundation at political events, it will flatten out into mere litany.

Even the verbal defense of the basic values remains weak and the appeals to the maintenance of the basic values will evaporate if they do not have a solid foundation of historical knowledge. However, if it belongs to the general knowledge that their importance was not only taken into account in Greek antiquity - which was no longer really democratic - and if it is already taught at school how basic values shaped social structures thousands of years earlier, how they led to the shaping of the common good in equal rights for all people, then we will be able to succeed in emancipating ourselves and our modern consciousness in the long term.

Then we will have the opportunity to expose verbal templates and ideologized constructs, and to counter the feelings of worry and powerlessness of an up-and-coming decay of our civilization with the knowledge existing at the very beginning of the history of human coexistence, when there were no nations, no borders, and no forms of governmental organization.

So it is about re-finding an attitude from which responsible action arises. This is why our essay deals with the origin of the basic values and pleads for taking joint responsibility for their preservation.

In 2019, we illuminated the principles of the egalitarian societies of Old Europe and reflected them briefly and concisely into the present by means of the following terms: basic values, common good, responsibility, democracy, equality, education, balance, nature, narrative, possession, work, satisfaction, homeland, connection, competition, trust, solidarity, authority, language, love, festivals, religion, and art as a stimulus to re-thinking. (LaBGC and Haarmann 2019, English translation 2021).

Now we are looking for clues as to how the primacy of the basic values shaped the communal sense of community and led to the egalitarian societies of the first high culture mankind has ever seen, Old Europe. We strive to trace the development in its entirety and to make the emergence of human coexistence visible on the example of the heritage of Old Europe and available for our epoch.

Our search for traces is not necessarily limited to Old Europe, but rather shows the continuation of the Old European basic democracy in ancient Greece and its democratic models. In this manner, it also includes the Greek historiography, in which the circumstances of the formation of the community are mythically trimmed and ideas become clear about what keeps the world in balance and how this also affects the relationships existing between people one with another and together in society. Our essay is also focused on this metaphorical meaning, social life in balance.

Even if some things may seem utopian, the historical dimension makes clear what was there at the very beginning and what is also possible in the future. Rutger Bregman excellently justified his "Utopien für Realisten" (2017) by mentioning examples coming from history. However, we go further back in the historical development by shedding light on the history of the alleged utopias. To deal with an epoch which, according to the traditional view of history, is still associated with the "dark" age means historical realism and a vision for realists.

However, this epoch may be all but dark! Let us look together into the earliest history and what followed and let us realize the importance of the basic values to shape democratic structures!

In this manner, we will be able to strengthen ourselves against attacks on the foundation of human coexistence and, guided by reason, we will get the chance to stand up for social balance and to assume responsibility.

1.   Trust, basic values, common good

The basic values have been practiced in cooperation with each other. And this is also the case today. The social behavior is the context in which basic values become aware and the responsibility for each other matures. The basis of the maturation process is trust and a sense of responsibility for each other as an expression of a basic attitude of solidarity, and this is basic attitude is a pre-political one. The whole thing results in basic democratic behavior, a focus on the common good and the realization that the well-being of all also ensures the prosperity of all – as it was the case in Old Europe.

This is the exact reason why we should note the following: The social and cultural development of the human species has its roots in the basic values. Listings of basic values exist in many formulations and in many contexts. There is no generally binding breakdown or separation of all possible basic values. Some prefer overarching, blanket content descriptions, while others prefer detailed specifications. However, it is certainly easy for all viewers to identify with the following overview:

- the equality of all people (in the sense of equal treatment despite anthropological, cultural or other differences between groups and/or individuals);
- the equality of all people before the law (be it the national legal system or the interconnection system of international agreements and conventions);
- the self-realization of people, as individuals and as members of social groups (free choice of residence, free choice of higher education, freedom of expression, self-determination at the

political level, participation in the political decision-making processes; right to vote in a democratic order);

- the gender equality (without any restrictions, neither in the private nor in the public sphere; free choice of the own spouse);

- the free movement of people to pursue their own economic interests (in accordance with the principles of a social market economy). Respectfully we call these five basic values the Big Five, just as one speaks of elephant, giraffe, rhinoceros, hippopotamus, lion, the large animals of Africa, the Big Five, demanding respect. The said metaphor fits, because we know that the more undisturbed the Big Five can unfold in their spheres of action, the more stable the balance of forces in the natural – and in the case of basic values – in the social environment will be.

For philosopher and business ethicist Christoph Lütge, the anchoring of basic values in society is part of an ethics of order (see Lütge 2007: 25 et seq.). In his approach to describing what holds a society together, Lütge sums up the essentials as follows (see 2007: 74 et seq.):

- The society needs common values (material value ethics);

- The society needs a common image of the human being as the basis for virtues;

- The society needs a rational motivation to assume ideal roles, capable forms of life and constitutional patriotism;

- The society needs a sense of justice;

- The society needs internalized dispositions for cooperation;

- The society needs common feelings of compassion and solidarity;
- The society needs a work ethic and an ethos of saving (in the sense of not wasting).

- Rights, obligations and responsibilities

In fact, the ingredients of a democratic order can be found here. An order of this kind is demanding, because it requires every citizen to maintain a balance between fundamental rights, fundamental obligations and a sense of responsibility through the own commitment to the common good. A balance of fundamental rights and a sense of responsibility in the sense of the common good corresponds to the consensus according to which people act in solidarity and activate the ability for coordinated cooperative action, completely, as the philosopher Jean Staune describes it, within the meaning of the so-called collective intelligence (see Staune 2019). The collective intelligence is effective if the common good of a society, in a balance of constructive forces, makes sense for all individuals by retaining its meaning.

The idea of a society with an interconnected system of basic values and common good based on trust, reflected in a democratic legal system with state bodies which also look at the compliance with the fundamental rights, awakens a sense of general well-being. Obviously, however, the compliance with the fundamental rights is not securely anchored in the agendas of state institutions. And the appeals addressed to the state institutions to care of these concerns fade away too easily. The inequality of what should in reality be equal has become a circulus vitiosus, and a growing drift apart.

The cultural scholar Aleida Assmann reiterates the need to confront human rights and human duties and to reconcile them by concluding that we must mobilize our "personal sense of responsibility" and take on the responsibility of our social behavior, so to speak at the "grass-roots level" (see Assmann 2018a). Just as there are the Big Five on the side of fundamental rights, they also exist when it comes to the fundamental duties with a sense of responsibility showing numerous facets:

- Mindfulness in dealing with others;
- Empathy, participation in the issues of others and tolerance towards other ways of thinking and living;
- Solidarity with others, basis of trust for the purpose of a concerted problem-solving;
- Willingness to cooperate in the implementation of municipal tasks and projects on their own responsibility;
- Priority of the common good over materialistic (one-sidedly individually oriented) profit-seeking.

  And precisely at this point it is important to respect the right of every person to housing and life-sustaining basic care.

- **Social commitment**

In his call "Time of Outrage!", Stéphane Hessel has put in a nutshell which central role the mobilization of the sense of responsibility plays in times of crisis. Hessel was a leading figure in the French resistance movement during the German occupation in World War II. The National Council of Resistance was founded in France in 1943 as an alliance of representatives of the resistance movements, political parties and trade unions and had written a program for a renewal in

14

Europe. If the world of politicians had followed his proposals responsibly, it could have become a new Old Europe.

"It is precisely these principles and values which are more necessary to us today than ever. We are all called upon to preserve our society in such a way that we can be proud of it: not this society of those pushed into illegality, of deportations, of mistrust of immigrants, in which old-age security and social security benefits have become fragile, in which the rich dominate the media - none of which we would have allowed if we had really felt committed to the legacy of the National Council of Resistance" (see Hessel 2010: 7 et seq.).

Stéphane Hessel was 95 years old when he wrote "Time for Outrage!" In his essay he warned of the imminent loss of basic values by calling for peaceful resistance. The awakening of society was also the objective pursued by Greta Thunberg, who at the age of 16 put the careful use of resources on the public agenda for the sake of the habitability of the planet for all. I want you to panic! This is what she said by explaining that it is high time for active responsibility. Children and young people all over the world imitate her. In this regard, the philosopher and historian of ideas Harald Seubert writes:

"High age and early adolescence signal a fundamental objection to organized processes, but also to an itineration of common political and academic rituals, even where they may generate added value in terms of knowledge, insight and information. What is common to Hessel and Thunberg is that at a certain point they do not ask for further discourses or facts, but for attitudes from which, according to the expectation, challenging actions then emerge. Age-related naivety of a teenager and of an old man? Not at all! Beyond pragmatic activities and common political compromises, the panicked basic mood is a signal to pause. This mood is the placeholder for the reorientation of attention to human interests" (see Seubert 2019).

While epidemics or pandemics evoke a rather egoistic behavior, because the other represents a potential danger, a crisis or even an obvious need for help is more likely to result in solidarity. In trust in each other and in the effect of joint action in the sense of the common good, often even starting from a spontaneous decision, outstanding examples of conscious implementation of responsibility at the local and municipal level emerge. If the examples of equally responsible people in a similar situation are taken up and adapted to the respective requirements of the given circumstances, further local initiatives are created, and they then spread regionally, transnationally and even across continents.

There are countless non-governmental and private initiatives which connect to networks and they do it especially to support people displaced by war. Here in the following, on behalf of many others, we will briefly describe three projects which have proven themselves over a long period of time.

- A project initiated in 1977 in the Netherlands with neighborhood buses, the so-called *Buurtbussen* skipped the country borders. In 1983, with the Bürgerbus in Münsterland in Germany, it became the first neighborhood organized help for mobility in German communities without sufficient public transport (ÖVP). Skeptics had given the initiative half a year, but it still exists, and the concerns have vanished because everyone benefits from it: small towns without public transport links are connected every hour. And this offers a great relief for families with young children and old people living in these communities (see Groll 2019).

- Another initiative which is worth mentioning is Buurtzorg, initiated in 2006 in the Netherlands by Jos de Blok. *Buurtzorg* is a neighborhood care and a program for sickness and old-age care, supported by local support teams. The initiative has no central administration since the local groups take care of their administrative needs by themselves. This results in savings of additional costs which would occur in a centrally managed organization. The members of each local team are residents of the neighborhoods in which they operate. This offers the advantage that the assisted people know them as neighbors. Teams of no more than 12 people ensure a flexibly coordinated deployment. In 2015, Buurzorg merged with Familiehulp, a family aid organization. In 2018, around 14,000 people worked in 1,000 teams, of which 4,500 were household helpers. The Buurtzorg formula attracted worldwide attention (see Gurny et al. 2018).

- With *housing first*, an American homeless project was adapted to Finnish conditions in Finland in 2007. Since then, the Finnish version of housing first, *asunto* ensin-malli, has been bringing people without their own accommodation into fixed housing conditions in a tightly knit network and has even been elevated to the rank of a national strategy. Underlying this is the realization that with a secure roof over one's head – which is a fundamental right – homeless people can get the chance to achieve social reintegration. The statistics prove the success of this project: At the end of the 80s, around 20,000 people were counted without own residence –

including those who do not have their own permanent residence and have found shelter with others – while in 2019 there were only around 4,000 homeless people in the country. This result was achieved through the interaction of locally organized aid and state support.

According to Juha Kahila, founder and head of the Y-Säätiö, Y-Foundation, the aim is that through housing first by 2027, all those who, for whatever reason, have no own accommodation, will re-obtain a permanent home and consequently dignified living conditions. Personal care plays a key role in this project in two ways, both in the provision of housing and in addressing the issues which have led to homelessness or have emerged from it. The challenge is to gain and maintain the trust of homeowners and those who need housing. The compelling results achieved in Finland triggered the establishment of further housing-first networks throughout Europe, in which experiences and suggestions are now exchanged.

What turns out at this point is the following: Trust, basic values and the common good are the pillars on which a sense of responsibility rests. This sense of responsibility becomes an inner attitude, a disposition, inscribed in the socialization process in the family of origin and in the groups while growing up, at school, during the training – an inscription that was given in the high culture of Old Europe from the experience of generations. The standard of living in Old Europe had been reached as an achievement in a cooperative society which was convinced of its basic values and focused on the municipal interests in the sense of the common good instead of individualistic aspirations to increase private wealth. This attitude could be transmitted for thousands of years unencumbered by armed

18

conflicts, which would have destroyed what had been achieved structurally or materially and ensured stability and security.

In Plato's political theory, we can find echoes of the cultural heritage of Old Europe. Plato inserted the common good as a cornerstone (see Haarmann 2017). Plato's achievement is that of enlightenment in the sense of an actual awareness of the essence of the common good. The fact that Plato wrote down the heritage of Old Europe sends a clear signal: the ancient Greek expression for common good, *to agathon*, is a loanword from the pre-Greek substrate, which was traditionalized from the language of the Old Europeans and got into Greek via the Pelasgian language (see Beekes 2010: 7). In Plato's interpretation of the notion of the common good, we are confronted with the reflection of basic rights, namely the fundamental duties of the individual towards other individuals and with reference to the state order as well as the importance of a sense of responsibility.

Not least through Plato, the legacy of the ancient high culture of Old Europe continued and continue to have its effects. And this happened by embedding all thinking in a spiritual framework, as it was characteristic of the world view of the people of Old Europe by having its modified meaning in ancient times. And so, according to Plato, each individual bears responsibility for his/her own salvation, and to do good is tantamount to a commitment to the good of the politically organized community to which the individual owes his/her personal well-being. This self-evident connection with the inexplicable may be strange to us, but it describes the assumption of responsibility for one another and the circumstances in which the coexistence takes place.

"Polis and soul should correspond to each other as the great and the small scriptures." This is the effective doctrine of Plato. Since only what is pre-marked in the small script of the soul, can be feasible and effective in the script of the large polis. Starting from this spirit, Hannah Arendt was able to renew a primeval form of democratic political action in which the free understanding of politics can be resolved out of totalitarian constraints to then be established in the freedom of speech and counter-speech. The conversation must not and should not break down even in case of dissent. The spark of the beginning, the nativity, which Arendt has renewed as a spark of democracy after Nazi fascism and totalitarian experience, must also be shown in the laborious processes of concrete consensus building. The normative of the polis is specifically grounded in one's own and in the other's soul. He or she may be right. Despite all the threats to commonality, despite all the inadequate realization, the awareness of a common good in which the various voices involved can combine to form a symphony remains fundamental. In this context, Derrida referred to the so-called 'politics of friendship'" (see Seubert 2019).

2. Timeline of Old Europe

In this chapter we investigate prehistoric times by focusing on the development towards – according to today's state of knowledge – the first high culture in human history. Its timeline includes the period from about 45,000 to 3,500 before common era. In a cursory view, we will describe the development of this high culture, the design of its communities and the essential aspects of its activity over the period of more than 3,000 years. Finally, we will explain how the transformation of high culture came about by pointing out the cultural and social-historical consequences that this had and still has in the further course of history.

- The formation

If we go back about 9,000 years from our present time, we see how, from what had proven useful and protective for generations, Old Europe emerged as the first high culture in human history and became the hub for collaboration, exchange and transfer of technology, creativity, beliefs, language and much more. The autonomy of this high culture compared to other early civilizations has been analyzed in a recent new paradigm of civilization research (see Haarmann 2020).

The part of Europe we are now primarily focusing on, with today's country names, includes the territories of Hungary, southern Poland, Croatia, Bosnia-Herzegovina, Serbia, Montenegro, Kosovo, Albania, North Macedonia, Greece, Bulgaria, Romania, Moldova, parts of Ukraine, the Aegean Sea and the Adriatic region. This wide area was the sphere of influence of the societies of Old Europe.

In this region, as everywhere else in the world, people began to live together in groups and communities because it was beneficial. Indeed, cooperation ensured survival. This was for example the case in the procurement of food, in finding or building adequate accommodation, in the manufacture of tools or clothing. Analyses of finds of human skeletons, of remains from fire pits and of excrement – all bio-historical documents – provide information about what women and men were able to procure from animal and plant food through joint hunting and gathering. The analysis of the finds also gives indications of habitation, clothing, even kinship and origin. Every further excavation, every refined investigation method, with which new finds are analyzed and old finds are analyzed once again, condenses the knowledge about lifestyle and mobility and migration movements.

And in Old Europe, as everywhere else in the world, people hunted and collected edibles. There was no gender-based division of labor. The division of labor developed only in the course of the Neolithic, much later than previously assumed, and was, as the anthropologist and archaeologist Steve Kuhn was able to prove, more a product of social norms than of biological or psychological circumstances (see Kuhn and Stiner 2006). The traditional argument according to which the division of labor is biologically given by the motherhood of women and limits the opportunities of women, and consequently the assignment and exclusion of certain areas of activity to women are quasi natural, is no longer tenable since "motherhood may steer the balance in one direction, but it does not close any paths. ... We must not forget that a good male as well as female hunter, or a good male as well as female collector needs a lot of knowledge and a high degree of skills. For women who are in the late stages of pregnancy or breastfeeding their child, it would be difficult and dangerous to go on a big game hunt. It would make sense for these women to develop other skills, such as those associated with the collection or processing of plant foods. Of course, when women passed childbearing age or were childless for other reasons, they could and did become skilled hunters." (see Kuhn 2020). The fact that women and men also went hunting is evidenced by rock carvings in Europe, such as on rock 24 in the vicinity of Nadro, Valcamonica, in northern Italy, in Minateda, in southern Spain, and in Brandberg, in Namibia, in southwest Africa, and recently also bone finds in the Andes dating back to before 8,000 (see Haas 2020).

Work-sharing processes emerged linked to the development stage of a certain society. As long as food procurement required the use of many people, division of labor was possible for the manufacture of tools such as hand-held equipment used for slaughtering animals and also for dismantling the carcasses and separating the fur from the meat. The meat was eaten, skins were used for clothing or in the construction and equipment of deposits, while bones became further, finer tools such as needles. Bones also became cult objects. All these types of work were based on the skills and were not determined by the gender of the worker. The results of the Paleolithic research show with what huge effort the daily life of the people was connected and that this could only be managed in the context of a well-coordinated cooperation. Consequently, it can be assumed that those of a community that proved to be particularly capable of organizing work processes were responsible for maintaining and developing the structures and processes which emerged and were viable.

-    **Plateau of impact**

In the vast regions of Old Europe, people had gradually become settled and lived from about 7,000 years before our age, predominantly in village communities, improved the cultivation of plants and the breeding of animals. No longer having to secure supplies by collecting and hunting edibles with a high level of human resources, the human being had released the own strength and creativity for agriculture and livestock breeding, the improvement of equipment and the development of innovative production processes. Now, utensils were also decorated and embellished. Furthermore, personal jewelry was made. Cult objects and figurines were created. They are all outstandingly proven for Old Europe and played an essential role in the coexistence of the people in Old Europe, in their cultural identity and in their whole sphere of activity. Furthermore, they give us an impression of clothing and hairstyle as well as of spiritual ideas and ceremonies today.

In the period between 7000 and 3500 B.C., some settlements and villages grew into cities having regulatory and social structures for more than 10,000 inhabitants. According to the actual state of research, the first writing and the first number system in the world was created. Ploughs for field work and carts for the transport of alumina were constructed, kilns for ceramics were built, the first pottery wheel was built, metal melting processes were developed, copper and gold were worked, and after boats the first ships were built.

The people of the high culture of Old Europe were enormously creative and productive, exchanging products, ideas and conceptions with each other, with neighboring settlements, as well as on long commercial trips – to the Atlantic in the west, to southern England and the Baltic States, to the steppe of southern Russia, to Anatolia and North Africa – brought new products, new conceptions and ideas, which were passed on again in the network of contacts. All helped to shape this cycle in a responsible manner and everybody benefited from it. Since the common good was the obvious orientation in thinking and acting and guaranteed stability, development and prosperity (see Illustration 1).

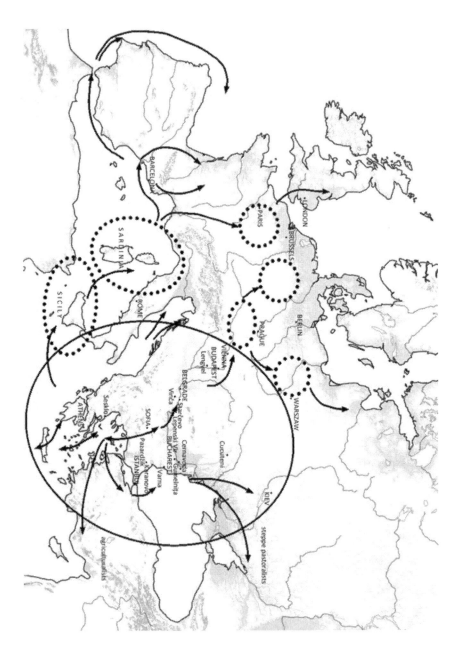

Illustration 1: The heartland of Old Europe and the interconnection of
the economic area: routes of domestic trade and external contacts

For more than 3,000 years, these communities prospered in harmony with nature – interdisciplinary research has so far found no evidence of any kind of exploitation – and without the experience of war and destruction. There were no demarcated empires or claims of one group to the territory of another group. The land was common property for the benefit of the people living and working there. In wide-ranging trade – goods were exchanged for goods, money as a means of payment did not yet exist in this cycle – the highly developed products from Old Europe were in demand and, conversely, trade brought home the raw materials and new materials needed, mainly under the responsibility of female traders.

With each return, the descriptions of what the merchants had seen and experienced during their travels and in their personal trade contacts certainly spread. As a consequence, not only animal skins came along from the trade trips to the steppe in the northeast, but also very conceivable remarkable things, such as the descriptions of stelae made of stone, which were not yet had in Old Europe, and certainly also of men who rode on horses, animals which were completely unknown in Old Europe. Conversely, the steppe dwellers were probably amazed by the tools made of metal, and they certainly saw objects made of gold for the first time. This was food for thought. The access to it promised power and wealth.

-      **Transformation**

In this manner, in the north-eastern region of Old Europe, in the transition to the steppe of present-day Russia around 4500 before common era eventually became a smoldering, which over the next

1500 years became a wildfire and gradually transformed the millennia of peaceful coexistence, which culminated in 3000 years of high culture. This was the most dramatic turning point in human history.

We can imagine it this way (see LaBGC 2020: 13 et seq.): As the first wave of immigration from the steppe, small groups of Indo-European affiliation gradually reached the territory of Old Europe. The route led across today's areas from Moldova, Ukraine, and Romania to Varna, in present-day Bulgaria. There one was certainly amazed at the men on horseback since until then they were only a vague idea based on the stories of the merchants, whose trading area was in the steppe. Was there a fearfully respectful admiration for the riders on the big animals and even dreams of riding a horse? This may be assumed. The Indo-Europeans settled down. This was nothing unusual for the growing city, where many came to learn and eventually stayed. The people of Varna understood this well, because their city was a successful hub for the exchange of goods, knowledge and experience. However, unlike other immigrants coming from other parts of Old Europe, those from the steppe had grown up in completely different structures.

Their societies were organized patriarchally-hierarchically, led by the supreme commander of a clan with glorious warriors and recruited from skillful horsemen among the shepherds, who increased their fame with the conquest and defense of pastures and waterholes. And there was a troop reliably acting in compliance with the given orders. And what about women? Women were subordinate.

Was there an element which pointed to the other socialization of immigrants and their pursuit of power, fame, and wealth? Probably, there was. However, the question arises: How should people directly recognize such a thing as threatening, if for them power and wealth represented no value at all? And if such a contradictory world view was completely foreign to them. Those who had no ruler but chose women and men as spokesmen for the municipal council, who were honest and reliable with prudence and foresight for the good of all committed authorities enjoying high reputation.

The clans gained the control of the trading center Varna and of the areas where they settled – still without any signs of destruction. Over the course of a few generations, the Indo-Europeans gained the upper hand in this merger process. The egalitarian order, oriented towards the common good, was gradually enforced with patriarchal hierarchical structures. The first groups of Old Europeans left their homes and emigrated to areas where no Indo-European had yet penetrated. First, they moved along the Danube in the direction of today's Vienna.

The second wave rolled out of the steppe between 4100 and 3800 before common era. However, this second wave was not deliberately approximating as it was the case for the first one, but determining and repressive. Why did the remaining Old Europeans not resist? How can we expect this from people who continued their lives without any destructive intentions? In addition, defense would also have had to turn against those women who, now living together with Indo-Europeans, no longer had their place in the circle of the family of origin, but in their partner's clan. Instead of the previously valid matrilocality, the patrilocality of the Indo-Europeans was now valid – women had to leave their families of origin and move into the family of men when joining a man. The patriarchal society of dominance gained further space. Oppression became repression.

Even the goddesses, great power in the mythical-cultural fabric of Old Europe, were in the end preceded by male deities.

Many large families of Old Europe set out to resettle in areas where the indigenous population was still Old European. These large families moved in all directions of Central Europe, and in the course of the third wave of Indo-European immigrants, which now started, they transferred their possessions in southeastern Europe to the Cyclades, which had been inhabited since ancient times by people of Old European affiliation, such as those who were later referred to as Minoans.

Not only in northeastern Europe, weapons were now also forged from metal. This made the third wave of immigration from the steppe between 3200 and 2800 before common era – for those people who did not want to be displaced, as well as for their peaceful culture.

In 1989, the prehistorian, archaeologist and anthropologist Marija Gimbutas was asked about her excavations in Old Europe and answered:

"Weapons, weapons, weapons! Unbelievable how many thousands of pounds of these daggers and swords from the Bronze Age were found. That was a cruel period and the beginning of what is today - you turn on the television, and it is, on whatever channel, war, war, war."

The orientation towards patriarchal and hierarchical structures which emerged in the transformation of the Old European societies was subsequently consolidated by power-enhancing narratives and power-preserving measures, elaborated to secure rule and elites. From the idea of a goddess as a great mother of creation, to whom men felt obliged by a treaty to preserve responsibly what was given to them, gods became as companions of different goddesses, few of whom retained a prominent position, until finally with monotheism the patriarchal principles of order were firmly anchored and since then were interpreted according to claims and aspirations for power.

And yet, in the coexistence of people, the primacy of basic values has survived. The importance of basic values in the consciousness of the political leadership of a country, its social groups, as well as in the consciousness of the individual is closely linked to the respective history. As different as the characteristics may be, it is the basic values connecting us.

3.   Civilizational achievements of Old Europe

This chapter fans out the elements set out i n a cursory view in chapter 2. The focus is now on the phase of the high culture between 7000 and 3500 before common era and the technical, architectural, cultural and structural achievements and on spirituality, which grasped everything unexplainable as in two semi-circles above and below a horizontal straight line.

-   Technological and cultural development

It is often proven that the people of the cooperative societies of Old Europe had developed technological knowledge and skills and complex organizational structures that were not realized anywhere else in the world during that epoch.

Around 5300 before common era, Old Europe has records on a world scale (see Haarmann 2020):

-      The first ploughs were constructed around 6000 before common era in order to facilitate the newly introduced, heavy work of field management.
-      Around 6000 before common era, the first seaworthy ships were built for trading on the Danube and its tributaries, after boats made of reeds, in order to extend the routes across the Mediterranean (see Haarmann 2018).
-      Processing of metal by means of special melting processes, from 5400 before common era for copper and from 4600 before common era also for gold. In the blacksmiths of Old Europe, tons of copper were melted down, and the oldest artifacts in the world were made of gold.

- Two-story houses were built and monumental architecture was also realized.
- A writing technology and a notational system for writing numbers were created. The writing system used is the oldest in the world and at least one and a half thousand years older than the ancient Egyptian or Sumerian script (see Haarmann 2010). The Minoans developed the script of their ancestors further to the so-called Linear A, from there the Old European Linear A came back to the mainland, where meanwhile the Indo-European language dominated, and in adaptation to the new idiom the Linear A was converted into Linear B.
- The settlements were predominantly of a village character. During the 5th millennium before common era, the first cities emerged. Some of them were between two and four times larger than the early cities-built Mesopotamia in the course of the 4th millennium before common era.
- The multitude of female figurines expresses an abstract art aesthetic that has been taken up again in modern times by artists such as Constantin Brancusi and Henry Moore and has shaped modern art (see LaBGC and Haarmann 2019: 147 et seq).
- Models of terracotta sanctuaries, miniature altars, and cult vessels, some of them inscribed and decorated with symbols, give us important insights into the differentiated spiritual life of the people of that era.

What did not yet exist in Old Europe, probably because it was not needed, were the political boundaries. The people of the different regional cultures interacted in a conflict-free environment.

The connecting elements among them were trust, basic values and the desire to secure a livelihood for all. Similar social structures and cultural traditions, and above all common economic interests resulted in the growing prosperity of Old Europe. The extensive trade relations first took place through the large waterway Danube and its tributaries, which is why Old Europe is also referred to as the Danube civilization, and finally also maritime, first in the Aegean and the Adriatic, then far into the western Mediterranean (see map 1 in the introduction). Important trading centers were Vinča (south of present-day Belgrade), Turdas in Romania and Varna in Bulgaria.

The partners in this trading network conducted their transactions in an atmosphere of mutual trust. What would the point of political boundaries have been in this context? It is this basic condition that makes it clear how it can be that the trading network at that time was able to achieve a truly international expansion. Indeed, it reached as far as Anatolia and as far north as Poland to the Baltic State and in the west through Central Europe to France and southern England. The trade route from the coast of the Aegean Sea to Italy and France to Spain stretched over 3,000 km. This route can be easily followed by the spread of one of the then coveted merchandise. The Spondylus shells from the coasts of the Aegean and jewelry made from them found their way to France (see Séfériadès 2009), and the spread of figurines of Old European provenance is also evident. On the one hand, the merchants brought it with them as a link to the goddess as a great mother and protector of creation, but certainly also because of the demand, which is consequently proof of the spread of a similar spiritual worldview. The figurines also served as a sign of the solidarity of the trading partners. They were ritually broken, and

35

the fragments remained with the partners (see Chapman 2000), which according to today's understanding corresponded to a contract.

The trade was localized and controlled at a communal level, and the gain acquired in barter was distributed according to the needs of a municipality within the community. Certainly, especially successful merchants, mainly women, had a special reputation, because they made a special contribution to the common good. Certainly, in the regions of the Danube civilization there was also a competition between individuals or groups, such as for privileges such as privileges over local markets. However, if this had led to merchants creating a trade monopoly to build up personal wealth, then this could be reconstructed on the basis of the archaeological traces. However, no differences can be seen in the size and floor plans of the houses themselves, and in no settlement, no district were houses found that were richer than other buildings or that stood out from others through a conspicuous hoarding of valuable goods (see Helms 1992). The distribution of copper objects does not show private hoarding, but on the contrary, these objects indicate an effective, communally controlled distribution network. Only in the case of ceramic vessels that were not intended for everyday use, sometimes extravagant forms and the careful execution indicate their function as showpieces and as a consequence a special social role of those in whose house these objects were found.

"Such complex contours and forms speak for a rich and perhaps socially competitive world of households, family celebrations and rituals that drew potters from different communities into a force field of interaction and competition" (see Lazarovici 2009: 158).

Traditional research had long assumed that the emergence of a civilization must be related to the formation of a state, as in the well-researched and well-known civilizations of Mesopotamia and Ancient Egypt (see Albertz et al. 2003: 8 et seq., 131 et seq.). For the settlements of Old Europe, however, no form of state organization can be proven. The equation 'early civilization = early state' can only be proven in the Ancient Near East, but not in Europe, which had long led to the miscalculation that the Neolithic societies of Old Europe could not be a civilization.

Today, archaeologists, anthropologists and cultural scientists also have extensive knowledge available about other civilizations of the world, for the early stages of which a state order is either not detectable or where such an order is only rudimentarily developed (see Haarmann 2011b: 83 et seq., 2020: 101 et seq.). For this reason, early civilizations necessarily and logically include old high cultures such as the ancient Indus civilization (see Maisels 1999: 186 et seq.) and the Danube civilization (see Haarmann 2011a). And the high importance of pre-Greek cultures and their state of development compared to Greek civilization has long since been proven, for example by the anthropologist and archaeologist David W. Anthony who stated: "Generally speaking, the Bronze Age Greece is understood as the first European civilization, ... Much earlier than is generally accepted, South-Eastern Europe has reached a level of technological skill, artistic creativity and social complexity that contradicts common perceptions" (see Anthony 2009: 53).

- **Egalitarian social order**

Of course, when people settled in the transition from the Mesolithic to the Neolithic, they did not fundamentally change their habits and mores, but kept what had proven useful for their safety and well-being and integrated it into the change and new conditions and circumstances of their community. The principle of egalitarianism of their experience gained over thousands of years in the joint procurement of food in hunting and gathering and providing food, the production of first equipment, finding and securing accommodation, the production of protective and warming clothing remained a priority in the organization of their way of life within their settlements. The question of who benefited from the surplus from agriculture and trade can be clearly answered for Neolithic Old Europe. The surplus was evenly distributed among all parts of the population and among all settlements. This means that the communal availability of resources in an egalitarian structured society could be guaranteed. According to the current state of knowledge, it can be established with certainty that the societies of Old Europe were egalitarian societies.

There was also equality between the sexes. All working operations to be carried out were divided according to skills and personal responsibility, without men dominating women or women dominating men. In some areas, it can be assumed that men and women were equally involved in the work process even if they executed different tasks. As a consequence, the researchers largely agree on the assumption that, for example, the high-quality ceramic with differentiated ornamentation, as it is known from the local culture of Cucuteni in Romania, is the work of female potters (see Lazarovici 2009: 134). We can start from the assumption that men were responsible for mining and transporting the appropriate clay for which carts were to be made, and for firing the clay in specially developed kilns.

Archaeology offers a particular body of evidence which negatively reveals egalitarianism existing in society. In the settlements of the Old Europeans, the characteristic features of elite rule and hierarchy were lacking:

- The grave culture of Old Europe does not make any distinction between rich and poor, that is, grave goods are distributed equally and do not show any social class differences, nor do they show any status-related differences existing between men and women;

- There are no typical domination insignia such as status symbols such as scepters or artifacts with a heraldic-symbolic function to identify belonging to a clan having a leading role;

- The layout of the settlements lacks floor plans for larger buildings which may be identified as the homes of chiefs or members of a social elite, and that would be richer equipped than other homes. There are also no demarcated districts whose layout would indicate residential districts belonging to an elite. The archaeological traces in the settlements reveal the absence of any social hierarchy, and even in the mega-settlements of the late times, in the cities of the Trypillya culture, no distinction is made between rich and poor households (see Chapman 2009: 85 et seq.).

- There are no ceremonial buildings demonstrating secular power, such as palaces;

-   There is a lack of evidence of control bodies as guarantors of political power, that is, there is no evidence of the existence of any warrior elite protecting a ruler. The first armory in Varna around 4500 before common era is associated with the first wave of Indo-European cattle nomads coming from the Eurasian steppe (see Haarmann 2012).

The sum of these negative factors – it is said the collective lack of essential indicators for a social elite and the non-existence of a hierarchically structured social order – confirms the egalitarianism as a constant in the design of the social structures in the Neolithic Old Europe.

The social development within the communities of Old Europe refutes the long-time prevailing view according to which hierarchies necessarily arise in the context of a high culture. It is only through the accumulation of power and the establishment of patrilocality, in which women leave their families of origin and move to those of men, as well as the security of men to pass on the inheritance to their own biological children, that an ideology of control over women sets in, as explained by the anthropologist Maria Cintas-Peña in an interview on an as yet unpublished research project. "There is no single cause, but it is processes with different ingredients that cook slowly. However, it is clear that inequality is a cultural process, there is no biological determinism" (see Cintas-Peña 2021).

Evidence of the emergence of inequalities during the Bronze Age in southern Germany, documented for a period between 2200 - 1500 before common era, shows the connection with patrilocality. For the first time, researchers were able to use archaeological investigations of the bones of a large burial field in the Lech Valley,

40

southern Germany, to read out family trees spanning four to five generations. The team of Philipp Stockhammer of the Ludwig-Maximilians-Universität München (LMU), Johannes Krause of the Max Planck Institute for Human History in Jena, and Alissa Mittnik of the University of Tübingen found only male kinship lines with sons of women who had come into the family from a distance between 400 and 600 kilometers. This suggests that when girls reached their fertile age, they had to leave the community. If they died earlier, they were buried with grave goods like the other close relatives, who were given weapons and detailed jewelry. Among all the dead without grave goods and all coming from the region there was nobody related to the family.

"Unfortunately, we cannot say whether these individuals were servants and maids, or perhaps even some kind of slave. What is certain is that through the male lines the farms were inherited over many generations and this system was stable for over 700 years. The Lech Valley shows how deep in the past the history of social inequality within individual households goes back" (see Mittnik et. al. 2019).

The study impressively confirms that we humans originally lived in equality and that inequality only arose in the time of the transformation of the egalitarian societies of Old Europe.

- **Large family, village community, and city**

During the epoch of Old Europe, when settlements had grown into villages and cities, when work processes were diversified and divided, a more differentiated coordination was necessary to organize life, work and trade in the municipalities in a compatible way and for the benefit of the entire community. The land was not private property, but belonged to those who inhabited and cultivated it. It was administered in the village community and in the residential districts of the towns in the civic council by elected women and men, who exercised their function temporarily and had no special rights or preferences as in a voluntary position. The decisions on the leasing and use of land were based on the well-being of all residents of the village, the district or the city.

Resources were available locally and such as the surplus of crop yields and goods exchanged on trade trips they went evenly to all sections of the population in all settlements (see Haarmann 2013: 78 et seq.). The concept of the egalitarian social structures-oriented self-government in Old Europe was *kome* and this expression belongs to the oldest layer of loanwords from pre-Greek times (see Beekes 2010: 814). The *kome* model worked so well that it spread in all directions through the hub of Old Europe with its numerous trade contacts and was also maintained by the Indo-Europeans, but without the hitherto obvious participation of women.

Within the communities of the villages and cities, the people lived together in large families and clans. This is shown by the floor plans of the houses and the arrangement of the buildings in the settlements of Old Europe. The fact that the family and not the clan was the elementary social grouping can be noticed, among other things, from the fact that the households were separated from each other in family size. Long houses with accommodation for entire families, as is characteristic in many traditional cultures, did not exist in Old Europe. The village community, *kome*, consisted of the housing complexes of the individual families. These were a few houses or a larger number of buildings with living and household rooms, workshops, and stables for the livestock. The one- and two-story houses were in some cases so tightly grouped that some residential complexes could be considered modern condominiums (see the Illustration 2).

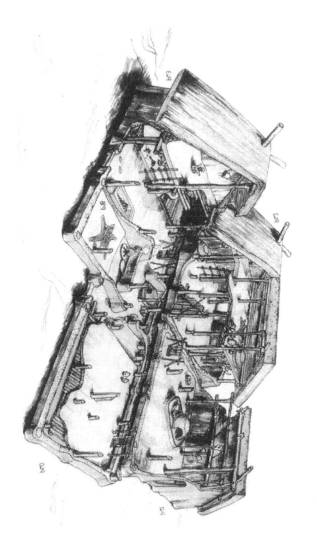

Illustration 2: The "condominium" of Parța, Banat (see Lazarovici et al. 2001: 257)

The characteristic of a *kome* was that the settlements designated in this manner were not surrounded by fortifications. This proves once again the peaceful life conditions of the settlement communities. There was no need to fortify settlements because there were no armed conflicts.

Not infrequently, a residential area was also assigned a temple reaching the size of the surrounding buildings, built on one or two floors like all houses with one or two rooms (see Gimbutas 1991: 327). A structure like this can be for example recognized in the plant of Truşeşti (Moldova) in the Prut Valley, a settlement of the Cucuteni culture going back to the 5th millennium before common era. The temples were presumably maintained by the clan of the respective residential complex and used for rituals to unite the clan and their connection with the great power of the goddess.

In order to stay with the family even after the death, the deceased were buried in groups. This is shown by findings of vessels with bone remains inside the houses. For example, during the excavations carried out in a house of the Copper Age settlement of Scânteia (Romania), an ossuary with a total of 111 bones and teeth of humans was found. The bones come from at least 33 individuals (see Bem 2007: 252 et seq.). However, there were also cemeteries arranged according to families, such as in Cernica (in the vicinity of Bucharest) (see Comsa/Cantacuzino 2001).

The clans of Old Europe were led by women. We can start from the assumption that these women, due to their special abilities, had the trust of all members. Grave goods confirm the leadership role of these women, as exemplified by the following description of a find of the regional culture of Lengyel in Hungary:

"Interesting are pearl belts made of marble or shells, which sometimes appear around the waist of women, most often those of the

45

age category "maturus". This jewelry can possibly be seen as an attribute for the "mother of a clan" and the pearls can consequently symbolize the numerous offspring left behind by the woman" (see Cermáková 2007: 254).

The leadership position given to women in egalitarian societies by their clan was confused by some researchers with female dominance and interpreted as a concept of matriarchy. This resulted in misunderstandings and conceptual discrepancies. There can be no question of the dominance of women over men. The archaeological findings clearly prove that the concept of matriarchy does not apply to the cooperative, egalitarian social structures of the Old Europeans. Already Marija Gimbutas, who was the first researcher to reconstruct an overall picture of the social conditions of South-Eastern Europe in the Neolithic, and dealt with the topic of social gender roles, firmly opposed the concept of matriarchy. "Indeed, neither in Old Europe nor anywhere else in the world do we find a system of autocratic rule by women with a corresponding oppression of men" (see Gimbutas 1991: 324).

The polarized hypotheses about a prehistoric matriarchy on the one hand and a universal patriarchy on the other are both untenable (see Dashu 2005 and Marler 2006 on basic positions in research history). And even Hodder, one of the critics of Gimbutas, who led the excavations in Çatalhöyük for a long time in the 1990s and at the beginning of our century, identified the social order of the Neolithic society in Çatalhöyük within the meaning attributed to it by Gimbutas, namely as egalitarian with a centered position of women (see Hodder 2004).

For millennia, human societies have had a matrilinear structure. This also applies to the Paleolithic Old Europe and also to its period of more than three millennia as a high culture. Mobility between immediately adjacent clans or clans of other regions was given according to the so-called matrilocation which consisted of the phenomenon according to which young men moved, presumably already after sexual maturity, from their group of origin to another clan, with whose women they were not related by blood. These were usually clans into which uncles or brothers from the same original tribe had already moved. For the matrilineal clans, Gimbutas (see 1991: 324) coined the term "matri-clan ruled by collectivist principles".

Modern research, especially in the fields of paleontology and anthropology, provides support for a matrilineal social structure. "The early kinship relationships of man were matrilineal" (see Knight 2011). In the context of a recent research project carried out by the European Commission on the development of inequality between men and women, it was shown for the societies of the Iberian Peninsula that matrilocality did not pass into patrilocality until between 3200 and 2300 before common era. The director of the project, Marta Cintas-Peña of the University of Seville explains that this was a created social and cultural process "which consolidated an unjust system." And it all started with the fact that a woman no longer remained in her group of origin when she joined forces with a man but had to move to the man's family (see Cintas-Peña 2021). Leonardo García Sanjuán, co-author of the unpublished study, explains the concept of patrilocality by stating the following: "This practice is very important for investigating the early emergence of patriarchy, because when women leave their families and villages and

47

move into those of their husbands, they are released from the context of their family and the support of their relatives and friends and this makes them more vulnerable to oppression by the man and his family." (see García Sanjuán 2021).

For this reason, the patriarchal order is demonstrably not a primary principle of society. The transformation of the egalitarian order of Old Europe with patriarchal structures goes back to the hierarchically-elitistically organized patriarchy of the Indo-European cattle nomads (see Haarmann 2016) and solidified over several generations (see Chapter 2, Timeline of Old Europe, Transformation).

- **Authority versus power**

Until the power-hungry immigration of the Indo-Europeans, the egalitarian societies of Old Europe acted in a basic democratic manner. Leadership in a group or clan, a community or a district was entrusted to those who had acquired the trust of others because their skills, for example of organizational type, were beneficial to cohesion and good neighborhood and trade relations, and presumably also because they were pretty good at moderating discussions. Such trustworthy persons were given authority and leadership.

This form of social life – not only in Old Europe – was the result of a development of millennia without the institution of a state. Authority figures already existed in the archaic clan associations of ice age societies. According to the terminology used in anthropology, these authority figures are called "headmen". However, they have not to be confused with the head of a hierarchically structured clan called the "chief" who, as a chief, has the power to enforce his will among the followers when needed. A headman – or headwoman – coordinates the interests of the group based on the authority granted to him or her by the group itself.

In great contrast to an elite position of power, authority – this still applies – is not hereditary, but tied to the actions of the person to whom the said authority is assigned by others. A son or daughter of a ruler follows in the reign, so inherits it. The descendants of an authority person cannot adopt the image of their father or mother, unless they themselves develop a personality with authority qualities and gain the trust of the group through their own achievements and are elected to a leading position. This does not mean that not even a person in a position of power can have this form of authority.

"The crucial difference between authority and power lies in the ability to control. Authority works mainly through conviction and example, and through tradition. Power does not exclude these factors but exerts domination through coercion. The measure of power is the sanctions it may impose. Sanctions are understood to mean the mechanisms of restrictiveness and punitive social control available to the powerful" (see Donlan 1997: 40 et seq.).

The high culture of Old Europe had neither a state bureaucracy nor territorial borders. The village settlements, as well as the early cities emerging in the eastern regions of Old Europe during the 4th millennium before common era in the area of Cucuteni and Trypillya culture, were based on self-government with a local council with a mayor as its board. People knew each other in the communities, and those who had acquired authority based on special skills and integrity stood out and were predestined to be elected to leadership positions. However, this authority-related position could also be withdrawn at any time. The authority that is meant here has no means of enforcing self-interest but acts and convinces in terms of example and leadership. If the persuasive power is no longer given due to lack of the example character, then the trust in the person will disappear together with its authority.

For a long time, it has been stated that complex societies develop hierarchies and the exercise of power. The complex societies of Old Europe with specialized crafts and specialized trade had extensive networks of social contacts and had the so-called complex social structures. However, this did not result in the formation of a hierarchical ranking of social groups. And even their Mesolithic hunting and gathering ancestors already had complex social structures: "Some regions offer good examples of logistically organized societies which are considered examples of 'complexity'" (see Spikins 2008: 9).

Therefore, authority and power differ in terms of the ways in which interests are enforced. In this manner, those in power, whether individuals or institutions, could negotiate or monopolize sources and distribution of economic resources among themselves and distribute or withhold these resources for their own advantage and, if needed and opportune, they could enforce them by means of physical control and also military force, just as the Indo-European leaders did with their warrior caste in Old Europe by imposing their hierarchical-patriarchal form of society on the communities having an egalitarian structure. In the history of the evolution of social concepts and social order, authority, and power stand in a clear chronological sequence to each other: Cultural history is primarily the form of authority accompanying the formation of trust, is based on basic values and acts by focusing on the common good.

-   Spirituality

For the sake of understanding, it is essential to know that just as there were no states distinguishing themselves from other states, there were no religions distinguishing themselves from other religions.

In the imagination of human beings, the great mystery of the origin of the earth and of heaven, of becoming and passing away, was a feminine one whereby this was not just the case for the people of Old Europe. Countless cave paintings, rock paintings and sculptures from the long prehistoric phase of mankind prove this from the Old Palaeolithic more than 500,000 years ago to the Middle Palaeolithic 100,000 to 40,000 years ago to the Young Palaeolithic 40,000 to 10,000 years ago. Marija Gimbutas looked at them and devoted herself to the analysis of the finds from the latter phase as well as of the finds going back to the period of the Neolithic from 6,500 to 3,500, which was the epoch of the high culture of Old Europe.

For the human beings, the Great Mother Goddess as a cosmic giver and taker of life herself was able to renew herself in the eternal cycle of life, death and rebirth, legible by nature. In the Paleolithic art, we cannot prove the existence of any father figure. The explanation lies in the fact that the relationship between procreation, pregnancy and birth has not yet been seen. Only in the Neolithic period there are a few finds of male statuettes in settlements and burial places. However, the now understood male part in the procreation did not change the image of the goddess as the female creator of the world. The findings of male representations can be interpreted as God figures, but they are still obviously partners, companions, and brothers of the Goddess, who magically increased the life-giving power of the Goddess through the sexual act or her physical strength. "Female and male sexes were not divided in two in the Neolithic conception, but, on the contrary, generated in their fusion the energy required by nature for its renewal" (see Gimbutas, 1991).

Gimbutas has divided the various manifestations of the conception of the Great Divine Power into categories to be able to clearly represent them in their functions and symbolism, but has emphasized that due to the simultaneity and continuity of the aspects described, it is always a single deity:

- the goddess who with life-enhancing, life-sustaining and life-giving aspects embodies the generative forces of nature,
- the goddess who, as the goddess of death, represents the destructive forces of nature,
- the goddess of life renewal, who determines the life cycles of nature.
- the prehistoric male deities; but together with the neolithic finds of male representations of God, they make up only three to five percent.

The iconography with attributions from the field of animals and consciously used forms, with which people characterized the different aspects of the presented Great Power, is extremely diverse

52

and recorded in Gimbutas in detail in word and image (see Gimbutas 1991, German translation of 1996).

However, this diversity, which is also reflected in the names given to the Mother Goddess, did not result in any distinctions. Within the multiple contacts connecting the people in the pre-state period without borders, reinforced by the far-reaching trade journeys in the three millennia of the high culture of Old Europe, the different representations and denominations apparently had no separating aspects of any kind. Rather, there seems to have been a consensus that it was always about the same creative power because the general assumption was that there was just one creation.

In this publication we will just name a small number of the many names transmitted by Old Europe through myths and taken by the Greek language from the Pelasgian, the language of the descendants of the Old European people. These names are Gaia, the original mother of the earth, Hestia, who in the Greek mythology was made the daughter of Kronos and consequently a representative of the "second" generation in the genealogy of the gods (*Homeric hymn to Hestia*, Pindar in *Nemeen* 11,110), Themis, Demeter, Artemis and Athena. The customs with which these goddesses were worshipped in ancient times are described in chapter 5 in the section entitled Festivals and Rituals.

The powerful image of the Mother Goddess, who was believed to create life out of herself, had been so deeply rooted in the cultural memory of human beings over the millennia that it was even preserved in various manifestations in the monotheistic religions, and in Christianity as the Virgin Mary.

4.   Timeline of Ancient Greece

"When societies are in turmoil, historical comparisons are in demand" (see Dümling 2018). All those who are looking for models of democracy begin in Ancient Greece by starting from the assumption that the first democracy originated there – and are then disappointed. From a realistic point of view, the sobering insight into the shortcomings of all historical models of democracy emerges, from the political order of the Athenian state in classical antiquity to the many variants of democracy in modernity (see Held 2006 for what concerns the analyses of various models of democracy). In order to facilitate the search at least for the period of the Greeks, a cursory overview of the effort for democratic structures in Ancient Greece shall be helpful.

- Remains of the grassroots democracy of Old Europe

A democratic order is based on basic values. A state model of order without basic values is not a democracy. On the other hand, a state organization is not a necessary prerequisite for a democratic order. In this context, a terminological conflict arises. The term democratic is derived from democracy and the model of the Athenian state during the 6th century before common era. However, if, as set out in Chapter 2, the essence of the basic values as the basis for democracy was proven to have been effective long before Ancient Greece in Old Europe, this means that the democratic thinking developed long before the emergence of statehood, namely within the state-free space. Moreover, it developed – and this is of considerable importance – within egalitarian functioning communities.

Let us briefly recapitulate developmental history and cultural history, basic values and democratic principles were already socially influential for thousands of years well before the epoch of Ancient Greece. The research has ample evidence for the span of more than 3000 years of peaceful prosperity in the expansion of high culture in Old Europe and points to the continuation of parts of ancient European civilization into the late 2nd millennium before common era, that is, into Mycenaean-Greek antiquity.

The first, spatially limited convulsion of democratic principles set in 4,600 and 4,500 before common era with the first wave of Indo-European immigration of belligerent shepherds from the southern Russian steppe. It is the beginning of a radical change, a turning point in time when the hierarchical-patriarchal culture of the Indo-Europeans gradually dissolved the egalitarian structures. In this context, the replacement of the hitherto usual matrilocality by the introduction of patrilocality produced an accelerating effect. After having met a man, women had to leave their families of origin and move into the men's family. As a result, many people of Old Europe abandoned their homes and emigrated to areas which were still inhabited by people with an egalitarian, grassroots democratic orientation. With the second wave of immigration which took place between 4,100 and 3,800 before common era, migrants coming from the north reinforced the changes by the force of arms, while maintaining favorable organizational structures. And they were able to expand what they had already learned from the indigenous population in the fields of agriculture, crafts, and trade. Between 3,200 and 2,800 before common era, the transformation of the economic and social structure throughout Old Europe was largely completed. The turn of time finally led to the first state borders, established in Europe in the 2nd millennium before common era in the form of the first kingship founded in the Mycenaean city-states.

In the investigation of what remained from the era of Old Europe after the radical upheaval, the comparison of the language of the Pelasgians, descendants of the Old Europeans, with the language of Ancient Greece was particularly revealing. The Greek descendants of the Indo-Europeans were, according to the first proper names, Thessalians, Thracians, Illyrians and Mycenaeans.

-    **The reform work of Solon (594 BCE)**

Ancient Greece consisted of city-states and the associated village settlements, the so-called *demen*, located in the respective surrounding area. From a conventional point of view, the conditions of origin of the democracy movement in Ancient Greece are associated with the work of the first great reformer, Solon (638 - 558 BCE) (see Blok/Lardinois 2006). Solon worked in Athens and for the Athenians, and what is known about the history of the reform system of his time concerns only the Athenian city-state and the demen located in the surrounding area of Attica.

As a member of a respected aristocratic family tracing its family tree back ten generations and leading the mythical Heracles as his ancestor, Solon brought with him all the required conditions that predestined him to a leading position when he was elected chairman of the nine-member Areopagus, the Supreme Council in Athens, which also served as the Supreme Court, in 594 before common era. This privileged status was promoted by the patriotic speeches addressed by Solon to the Athenians around 600 before common era, when the Athenian city-state was involved in a war with Megara over the control of the seaport of Salamis and received much positive attention for this. According to the chronology of ancient Athens, in which the years were named after the annually newly elected chairman of the Aeropagus, the year 594 before common era is listed as the "Year of Solon" in the city history of Athens.

Solon could have turned his office into a "tyranny" – the term was still understood as "sovereign authority, sovereignty" – and become the sole ruler. However, the experience of the egoistic striving for power, the opportunistic manipulation and lack of freedom of the citizens was still in the memory of the epoch in which Cleisthenes (not identical with the later reformer) in Sikyon and Theagenes in Megara had expanded their sphere of power against the existing political resistance. And in Athens itself, in 632 before common era, Cylon's attempt to establish himself as a tyrant had failed. As a consequence, a few decades before Solon, the Athenians had certainly had experience with the emergence of sovereignty. And so, Solon's mandate in his election as chairman of the Areopagus was to prevent the possibility of subversion.

For his actions, Solon set the priority of bridging class differences and basing political responsibilities in the Athens state on a broader basis and creating guidelines for defusing conflicts of interest arising between the existing social classes. For Solon, the concept of *demo* was synonymous with *plethys*, simple people who were to be given a say in the state order in the context of his reforms in order to overcome the autocracy of the nobility. In no case, however, should the common people be allowed the power which might have enabled them to dominate the aristocrats. Solon was not concerned with abolishing the existing class distinctions, but rather with replacing the privilege of noble descent with the criterion of material prosperity, that is, with admitting the wealthy among the *plethys* as representatives of the People's Assembly and as members of the Council.

„… Solon paved the way for democracy during the 5th and 4th century before common era by replacing the [privileged] birth with wealth as a determinant of political power... Solon was as much a democrat as Plato was a Christian which finally means that Solon was not a democrat" (see Roberts 1994: 51).

Of course, all this only applied to men. Women were not up for discussion, and slaves were not.

After completing his reform work, Solon left Athens. Whether he ever intended to enable male representatives of the lower class, the thetes, to participate in the popular assemblies of the Aeropagus is considered unlikely (see Foxhall 1997: 131 et seq.). If such a privilege had been granted to them, it would have restricted the supremacy of the nobility and the wealthy classes and would have afforded the Thetes the opportunity to hold the aristocrats accountable and even to judge them, since, after all, the Aeropagus was the People's Assembly and the Court of Justice at the same time. A participation of the thetes would inevitably have resulted in the resistance of the upper class.

59

In this context, two aspects should be pointed out. First, Solon had inserted into his reform work parts of the legislation already in place in the city-state of Athens. It had been written by the city's first legislator, Dracon, and had entered into force in 621 before common era. Which laws other than the criminal law for murder and manslaughter, which is still common in the expression "draconian measures" in German, were adopted from Dracon's collection, is not known. Secondly, the thetes were admitted only in the course of the 4th century before common era as representatives of the People's Assembly and as council members (see Missiou 2011: 122 et seq.).

Solon's reform could have been a stronger revival of the core values of Old Europe and its basic democratic structures, but the fixed status differences in the Greek class society stood in the way. Solon's reform became a minor reform. In addition, elements were preserved which promoted elite rule. The access to public office continued to be linked to material prosperity, measured by the amount of annual agricultural production on land. It may be that this regulation was based on the idea of a financially and economically independent government official who does not run the risk of becoming entangled in dependencies on others and on their interests. However, Solon continued to promote the manipulation of political rule by ambitious aristocrats.

As a consequence, the progress made with Solon's reforms was modest, and by no means eliminated the risk of tyrannical usurpation of power. "The reforms made by Solon decisively set Athens apart from possible solutions to the problem of large-scale coordination in the style of Sparta, but they did not put an end to the danger of tyranny" (see Ober 2008: 58).

The final text of the law was interpreted in the Prytaneion, the meeting place of the council in the center of the city near the Agora and could in fact be viewed by every citizen. In practice, however, it was made more difficult to understand by a formal legal language with ancient language, which was only accessible to a few Athenians. Furthermore, reading and writing at that time was essentially the privilege of the wealthy upper class (see Thomas 1992: 66 et seq.). In short, the texts conceived by Solon could only be received by a tiny minority.

According to Herodotus' report (*Histories* 1.29), the Athenian state was obliged to maintain the new constitution for a duration of ten years. Aristotle, on the other hand, reported that the agreement referred to a period of 100 years (*Athens Constitution* 7.2). According to the research, the period of time mentioned by Herodotus is the realistic and historically correct one. However, after only four years, the old power struggle between the aristocratic families flared up again, and some of those who had come into office refused to resign after the end of their term of office. The short period of validity of Solon's reforms to defuse conflicts of interest between the social classes shows the lack of willingness of the privileged to put their actions at the service of the common good.

Solon had to come to terms with the realities of a class society, however hard he might have sought the balance. An elite, a minority of wealthy Athenians, all members of influential extended families or clans, continued to exercise their political control. Although Solon, as an intermediary between the classes, had succeeded in some weakening of the class differences, he had shied away from involving the lower strata of the population in the existing political decision-making processes. And so there was still no trace of egalitarianism as it was the case in the community of Old Europe. The introduction of hierarchy and patriarchal order by the Indo-Europeans had prevailed against the principle of a democratic order, as in the heyday of Old Europe.

-   Political reorganization by Cleisthenes (507 BCE)

In Athens, Solon's approach was valid when Cleisthenes started his reform. Although in Solon's way the experiments were made with various forms of rule in the other Greek city-states during the 6th century before common era (Robinson 1997), none of these were suitable for the democracy Cleisthenes wanted to achieve. He could only rely on the municipal self-government in the village communities, the so-called demen, which, although no longer with the participation of women, still worked in continuation of the traditional and proven fundamental democratic principles. Cleisthenes expanded their function by transforming the demen into the collective bearers of political responsibility for the state order. This function was also assigned to municipalities, namely districts in Athens. In fact, "clearly defined municipalities within the city of Athens were converted into demen, ..." (see Osborne (1996: 296 et seq.).

The demen order of the village communities of Old Europe, which as so-called *kome* had become a well-functioning system that the administration had placed in the hands of village councils – elected women and men – for many generations had also been maintained in the Mycenaean world of states, i.e. many hundred years before Cleisthenes whereby the essential difference concerned the exclusion both of women and slaves. And Cleisthenes also did not lead an equality debate. The equality was conceded exclusively to the free, male citizens of Athens. The democracy established in 507 before common era was a political model for the chosen people, which were a minority of Greek society at that epoch.

From this point of view, the three pillars of the Athenian democracy introduced by Cleisthenes should be considered:

- *isegoria* ("equality of speech")

  This concerned the right of every free Athenian citizen to speak freely about political matters and referred primarily to the right of representatives to speak in the People's Assembly (*ekklesia*).

- *isonomia* ("equality before the law")

  The principle of equality applied only to the free citizens and, above all, to men's rights, since the legal situation of women with the right to citizenship in Athens was significantly restricted.

- *isopoliteia* ('equality of political activity')

  This type of equality aimed at equal opportunities in the election of representatives for the People's Assembly and the holding of state offices, which was reserved for male citizens by excluding women. For women of the wealthy upper class, only the office of priestess in the state cult of the Athenians and in some other cults was possible.

To sum up, the period in which the Athenian state had an order based on democratic principles can be divided into two phases. The early phase, the so-called classical era, begins with the introduction of democracy by Cleisthenes in 507 before common era and ends with the beginning of the Peloponnesian War between 431 and 404 before common era. When the war with the rival Sparta breaks out, Athens is at the zenith of its political power and economic prosperity. The consequences of the war were devastating. Athens loses its former importance, and Sparta takes over oligarchs as vassals of influence in Athens.

The second phase begins with the successful uprising of democratically minded resistance against the so-called "30 tyrants" in 403 before common era by enabling the reintroduction of democratic structures. However, the weaknesses of the model established by Cleisthenes quickly became apparent. Demagogues and populists dominated the affairs of the state. The gradual decline began until the model of democracy under Macedonia's supremacy finally became meaningless in 321 before common era.

The supposed first democracy was not conclusive from the beginning, but a kind of Janus-headed democracy. This "democracy" did not know any principle of egalitarianism but relied exclusively on an elite principle, which was not really put into question by Cleisthenes himself. The social hierarchies remained, and the power structures continued to solidify. In this context, the view of *democratia* from the point of view of two contemporaries, the philosophers Plato and Aristotle, is instructive (see Chapter 6).

Trust, basic rights, and common good were not there for state reasons. And yet it is worthwhile to analyze the changes in detail.

5.   Transformation of the order of Old Europe

With their hierarchical power and possession-oriented patriarchy, which was initially introduced creepingly and ultimately by force, the Indo-European nomads, who had immigrated from the steppe, had left their mark on the hitherto egalitarian society of Old Europe. The remnants of the old grassroots democracy, which were advantageous for the Indo-Europeans, the *kome* organization, were preserved in the area which was still state-free. The only but substantial change was the exclusion of women from the election and consequently from the decision-making processes. Otherwise, the rules for the administration of settlements and villages continued to echo the truly democratically organized Old Europe, when the term *kome* was replaced by the Greek designation of *demen*.

–   The tribal league

The Indo-European Greek society had been divided into tribes in the course of the seventh century before common era. Each of the said tribes had a council of elected men, in which decisions for the tribe were discussed and made in continuation of the Old European custom by majority vote.

The term for tribal unions was *amphiktiones* (also *amphiktionia* and/or amphiktyonia), a term designating neighborhood relations and referring to the epoch of Old Europe. And also the Greek term amphiktiones *amphiktiones* and/or *amphiktuones* still has the meaning it had in Old Europe: inhabitants of the area, population in the neighborhood, border neighbors. It is a word composition from the preposition *amphi-,* which means around and the verb *ktizien*

65

which means dwell, settle, found, and is mythically transfigured in narratives about Amphiktion, the founder of the Delphic-Pylic amphiction (see Gantz 1993: 234 et seq.). In the mythical genealogy, Amphiktion is the son of Heros Deukalion. Stories about Deukalion are connected with Thessaly and also with the sanctuary of Dodona, whose founder Deukalion is considered to be. This is another indication of pre-Greek origins, as Dodona refers to the Pelasgians, descendants of the population of Old Europe. And as it was the case in the culture of Old Europe, all important activities of the public life in ancient Greece were accompanied by rituals and religious ceremonies.

At which time exactly the tribes first joined together as a federation to negotiate joint council meetings decisions is just as little known as the closer circumstances of the formation of the federation itself. Scattered references in historiographical works and in thematic processing in myths indicate a dating in the course of the 8th century before common era. Certainly, however, the amphictionia are a much older organizational form. McInerney (see 2000: 164 et seq.) associates the oldest identifiable organization of an amphictionia with Thessaly, because a Thessalian was the respective chairman of the tribal council. Consequently, we can start from the assumption that the initiative for which an alliance had started from the Thessalians and should provide for the establishment of a supra-regional security system (see Wüst 1954-55). For with the change from egalitarian to patriarchal culture with clans, chiefs and elite troops, there were always conflicts, which were at the same time a matter of demonstration of power. The weapons in the hands of the clans' troops, which had been forged in large numbers since 3,200 before common era, were used relentlessly in conflicts. In that context, a system such as a federation of as many tribes as possible, in which a council could help avoid disputes, was certainly a wise decision.

As a sanctuary of supra-regional importance, Anthela, the sanctuary of the pre-Greek goddess Demeter, first became the meeting place of the tribal covenants. Over time, this amphitheater expanded. Its geographical influence was extended by including Delphi, which eventually became the capital of Greece's most significant and influential supra-regional institution in the course of the 7th century before common era. All those who were involved in the Delphic network became Hellenes, an expression originally associated only with a part of the amphictiony (see Malkin 2011: 59 et seq.).

The tribal council of the Delphic amphictiony consisted of twelve tribes which all had two representatives. During the second century before common era, according to a report by Pausanias, the body of 24 council members had grown to 36 members (see *Dihegesis* 10.8.1-2). Although the individual tribes are listed in the sources, none of the lists is complete. However, if we compare the lists, we can gain the conclusion that twelve tribes were actually represented (see Hall 2002: 137).

The assembly of the whole council met twice a year, in spring and autumn, in Delphi, with council members also gathering in Delphi for sacrificial rituals and other religious festivities. The mission of the Delphic amphictiony was based on the following two principles:

-       Every tribe represented in the council had to observe the peace commandment and acts of war by one tribe against another were forbidden because all disputes were to be negotiated and settled in the council.

- Every tribe pledged to respect the supply of drinking water not only with regard to the settlements in its own area, but also in other regions and not to cut off any city from this supply.

  The principles reflect the apparently serious conflicts caused by acts of war and by the denial of access to drinking water.

The violations could be punished by sanctions. Three times in the history of the Delphic amphictiony, the majority of the congregation proclaimed the "holy war" against the respective tribe and its members who had violated the principles:

in 591 before common era, at the end of the 450ies before common era and between 356 and 346 before common era (see Hall 2002: 145 et seq.).

Particularly dramatic was the role of amphictiony on the eve of the invasion of the Persian army led by Xerxes. According to Herodotus' account (*Histories* 7.132.1), at the urging of the Thessalians, the majority of the representatives in the council voted to offer the Persian king earth and water which were the traditional symbols of submission. Athens and Sparta voted against it. Thus, the burden in the war against the Persians lay solely with the two city-states. Support came from cities which wanted to participate in the war against the Persians. These cities swore an oath that they would ensure with sanctions that part of the assets of the "collaborators" which were the tribes whose representatives had voted for the subjugation under Persian rule would be put as offerings in the Shrine of Delphi (see Osborne 1996: 339). Whether this principle was also complied with after the victory over the Persians is not known.

It has passed down that the interests and importance of individual tribes or city-states changed over the centuries in which the Delphic amphitheater existed. The presiding representatives of Thessaly in the Council used their position, for example, to keep the inhabitants of regions bordering their tribal territory dependent: either as *perioikoi,* economically dependent, or as *hypekooi,* limited self-employed. This means that there were times when the vote of nominally independent members of the Council could, due to particular interests and political dependencies, override the needs and interests of others as well as corresponding regulations.

This possibility is also shown by the act of the King of the Macedonians, Philip II, who usurped the presidency of the Delphic amphitheater in 346 before common era and stripped the council of its authority by subjecting it to his own political will. The representatives of many tribes left the committee, which had become meaningless. Among them there were the Athenians, who henceforth used the sanctuary Dodona to hold their meetings. The contacts between Athens and Dodona flourished for several years, but were abruptly interrupted when the wife Philips, Queen Olympias, informed the Athenian magistrate that Dodona was in the Molossia region, she was a Molossian princess, and the Athenians should no longer dare to desecrate the sanctuary of Dodona by her presence (see Stoneman 2011: 64). In other words, the mighty Olympia banned the Athenians.

The council of the tribes never recovered from these upheavals and eventually dissolved.

- **The demen order**

The democratic order introduced by Cleisthenes in 507 before common era was not a revolutionary innovation, not a real leap in world history. It is correct that Cleisthenes' model of rule was based on the existing structure of the tribes and the principles of agreements won in consultation inherited from the epoch of Old Europe. In fact, Cleisthenes had reclassified the tribes and regrouped the traditional distribution of the village communities among the old tribal areas. The division of the Greek population into tribes was maintained. However, the reorganization changed earlier spheres of political influence of clans within the tribes (see Jones 2004).

There are different assumptions about the reasons for the reform. Herodotus believed that Cleisthenes had fallen out with the Ionians and had endeavored to give the inhabitants of Athens a central role in the state organization (see *Histories* 5.69). Aristotle hit the heart of this matter in his *Politika* (1319b19-27). In fact, Cleisthenes was concerned with mixing the inhabitants of the Athens State in order to achieve greater coherence of political participation in the community building. Before Cleisthenes' reform, there was a marked polarization of aristocratic families according to their affiliation within the twelve tribes. With the reorganization, there were now only ten tribes and their also new territorial borders cut through the territories of the old ones. This meant new ethnic attributions for the demen. In this way, traditional blocs and influences of the long-established aristocratic clans were abolished.

The tribes also got new names, which were not chosen by chance, at least if one does not want to attribute the pronouncement

70

of the names by the Oracle of Delphi to chance. In her trance, the Delphic oracle priestess Pythia chose ten names from a much longer list (see *On the Athenian State* 21.6 by Xenophon). These names were familiar from mythical narratives about Heroes of Athens history and presumably conducive to the acceptance of the reordering:

-   Tribe I (the Erechtheis): Erechtheus was raised as an orphan by his foster mother Athena and ruled Athens as its first mythical king.
-   Tribe II (the Aegeis): Aegeus is one of the mythical kings.
-   Tribe III (the Pandionis): Pandion was also one of the mythical kings.
-   Tribe IV (the Leontis): Leos was the son of Orpheus, who sacrificed his daughter to the gods to redeem Athens from the plague.
-   Tribe V (the Akamantis): Akamas was included in the list of mythical kings.
-   Tribe VI (the Oineis): Oineus was the son of Porthaon and Eureite.
-   Tribe VII (the Cecropis): Cecrops is mentioned in the list of mythical kings.
-   Tribe VIII (the Hippothontis): Hippothoon was the son of Poseidon.
-   Tribe IX (the Atlantis): Atlas, bearer of the celestial vault, was the son of the Titans Iapetos and Clymene. His son is Prometheus.
-   Tribe X (the Antiochis): Antiochus was a mythical hero from Attica.

Each of the said tribes was divided into so-called "thirds". In the case of tribe III, for example, this meant that one third of the tribe area was composed of inland demen in the west, another third grouped the coastal demen while the last third included urban demen near Athens (Fig. 3).

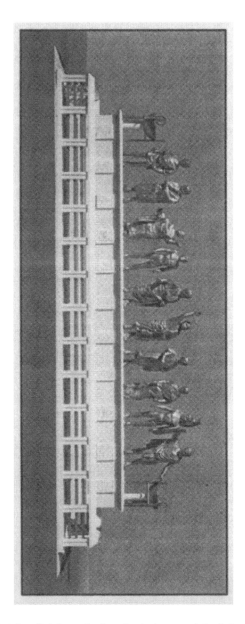

Illustration 3: The division of tribes in Attica: model of the monument of the eponymous heroes on the Agora in ancient Athens (see Lang 2004: 9).

The number of eligible male citizens of a *demos* was linked to the population. There were demen with only a single political representative, for example Hestiaia or Iphistiadai near the city of Athens even if the majority of the demen provided several citizens with voting rights. The highest number of representatives from the same *demos* was 11, for example in the case of Eleusis or Aixone. On average, the demen had three or four representatives. Approximately one-third of the demen was larger than the average, while two-thirds of them were average or smaller. Such proportions merely indicate the conditions of the inhabitants with regard to their Athenian citizenship.

Women, slaves and foreigners had no voting rights, for example merchants and seasonal workers who lived in the demen. For this reason, this group was not counted. Around 85 percent of the population of the Athenian state in the 6th century before common era were rural inhabitants. This aspect underlines the high importance of involving the demen in any structural change.

While the tried-and-tested form of self-government in the village communities of Old Europe called *kome* was characterised by elected women and men who were trustful because of their ability to act for the benefit of all the inhabitants of a village, the administrative bodies in the new communities called *demen* were exclusively occupied with male wealthy people who just wanted to assert their particular interests.

- **House, village and town**

The home of a large family was the *oikos*. This was a group of buildings with a dwelling house with space for a house altar, stables for cattle, workshops and a courtyard, where there was also space for a house altar or house shrine. The term *oikos* included the inhabitants, and these were usually three generations. Their slaves were counted among the inhabitants of a household, although they had no rights in the *oikos* . The slaves were divided into different categories: those belonging to the household community were named *oiketes,* the domestic slaves belonging to the property were called *ta oikeia* and those belonging to the family head were called *kyrios*, as documented by the epic literature of the 8th century before common era.

If one tried a purely socio-economic analysis of the ancient conditions, one would rather come to distorted or ideologically distorted results (see Kondylis 1987). What made an *oikos* – and also a *demos* – were not only aspects such as division of labor and productive power or the social conditions of existence. The essential aspect of the quality of life and consciousness was the togetherness in the extended family and in the village community and the spiritual world view. At least that hadn't changed since the epoch of Old Europe. In the sense of community in the extended family, the *oikos* was established as the general legal basis of the customary law and of the collections of laws of Dracon (621 before common era), Solon (594 before common era) and Cleisthenes (507 before common era). In the so-called Athenian democracy, the *oikos* was also understood as a political concept, namely as the supporting foundation of the state.

Derivatives of the oikos concept live on in many cultural languages: *oikonomia* for example in the German word Ökonomie, *economy* in English, *économie* in French, *oikologia* for example in the word Ökologie in German, *ecology* in English, *écologie* in French, *ekologija* in Russian, *oikoumene* in Ökumene, oecumene, oecouménée, ekumenija etc. The original meaning of all these expressions in ancient Greek differs from the modern usage. The term *oikonomia* referred to the basic rules of how a family household should be run, *oikologija* had to do with the living conditions in an *oikos*, and *oikoumene* was generally referred to as the ancient world inhabited by the Greeks. And this world was a polytheistic world. The later term ecumenism reflects the diversity in the coexistence of different religious communities.

How central the concept of the *oikos* was for the understanding of the Greeks is clear from many derivations (see Chantraine 2009: 753 et seq.). For example, *apoikia* "colony", a composition of *apo-* "away from" and *oikos*. For the Greeks of antiquity, a colony was a place far from home (see Malkin 2011: 53, 211). The verb *oikizo* meant the establishment of a colony. Settlements outside the Greek heartland have been identified since classical antiquity with regard to certain status criteria, and if one "in the 4th century [BCE] described a settlement as *emporion*, it was positioned in a solid political, legal and even social context" (see Wilson 1997: 200). The term *apoikia* referred to communal festivals with which the inhabitants of the Greek colonies on the shores of the Mediterranean and the Black Sea had ritualized their attachment to the mother cities.

Another derivation is also interesting: the term*metoikos* means "immigrant, foreigner" (*meta* + *oikos*). The *metoikos* is

76

literally "someone moving to another home". These were the immigrants or emigrants who moved from one place, such as their hometown, to another. The *metoikoi* in the Athenian state, immigrants or foreigners who lived among the Athenians, had come from outside, for example from the territory of another Greek city-state or from abroad (Phrygia, Thrace, Egypt, etc.), and had settled as merchants in city of Athens. The *metoikoi* had no Athenian citizenship and were consequently outside the legal protection of the Athenian laws (see Lape 2010: 46 et seq.). The *metoikoi* had to pay staggered taxes. There was a general tax for foreigners and a special tax for foreign merchants who did their business at the Agora. Athens citizens, on the other hand, did not pay any taxes.

About two millennia after the drastic change from egalitarian to patriarchal structures, the first city-states, the so-called *polis*, were established. The Mycenaean texts talk about the demen (as a translation of *demoi*, the plural of the word *demos* designating the "village community"). The aspect which remained largely the same was the following:

"... the settlements of average size - as in the Neolithic period - would have concentrated on the cultivation of cereals and legumes (which are labour-intensive, regardless of the extent of cultivation), as well as of some types of vegetables, and on livestock farming in limited numbers, whereas horticulture, the intensive use of livestock for secondary products [dairy products] and the cultivation of rare types of crops would have been practiced predominantly in large settlements..." (see Dickinson 1994: 51).

As it was the case in the epoch of Old Europe, during the Mycenaean rule in the 2nd millennium before common era, the demen were the economic and socio-demographic foundation of the regional states and the city-states. However, the structure was no longer egalitarian, but patriarchal. Among the representatives with seat and vote in the municipal councils there were no longer women. The autonomous self-government in the *demos* had become the monopoly of male decision-making.

The meaning of the term *demos* with its initially municipal-administrative orientation developed further and was then related to the community of the inhabitants of the settlements. In its expanded meaning, the term *demos* referred to the settlement community of an area or a district. The terms area and district with the associated local population imply the idea that according to which the territorial district in its area and the population living there are part of a larger whole.

"The demen resembled the city in miniature form. Every [*demos*] was self-sufficient to a certain extent because remnants of department stores and workshops were found in the demen. There were assemblies in every *demos*nominating a "mayor" *(demarchos)*and all other necessary officials, enacting decrees and laws, some of which have been preserved [chiseled] in stone. Taxes were levied to secure the reserves of a *demos*, and each *demos* had its own local cults and festivals" (see Bolmarcich 2010: 390).

In contrast to the era of Old Europe, in ancient times the inhabitants of house, village and city now clearly distinguished between free Greeks, women and male and female slaves. The fundamental change in the social structure with hierarchy and class division was firmly established. There is no echo of the social equality of all members of a dwelling as in the times of Old Europe in the Greek world of antiquity.

- **Municipal land ownership**

"Before the first democratic institutions and governments could emerge in Greece, a long process of social and intellectual development had to have taken place in order to build up the necessary political environment. The rise of the independently governed city-state, the *polis*, was one of the fundamental steps" (see Robinson 1997: 65).

Well, this fundamental step brought about a serious change: during the pre-state times - and before the turn of the times with the change from egalitarian structures to patriarchal-hierarchical ones – the land belonged exclusively to the people who lived and worked on it and was managed by consensus in the village community. With the establishment of the first city-states further property relations were added. There was an assignment to certain status categories (see Isager/Skydsgaard 1992: 121 et seq.). According to the temporal classification, municipal land ownership and the special status of sanctuaries as sacred land ownership are the oldest forms of ownership. With the emergence of states and borders, the state land ownership was introduced and included meeting places and theaters. A land ownership in private hands has been proven for the Mycenaean period, i.e. from about the middle of the 2nd millennium before common era. For this reason, the separation of individual land ownership from land ownership under municipal control is a secondary development in the social order – with the well-known socio-economic excesses which are particularly drastic today.

In the era of the Mycenaean city-states, officials with special powers were responsible for the relations between the palace bureaucracy and the demen, under whose responsibility the administration was, as archive texts by Pylos describe. A high-ranking official, the *damokoros*, represented the interests of the palace to the representatives of the demen, the so-called *damartes*. In this context, it should be noted that the derivation of the title *damartes* derives from the basic word *damos* from pre-Greek times (see Ilievski 2000: 148 et seq.), which once again shows the origin of the demen order from the Old European kome order and proves the continuity into the Mycenaean period.

Municipal land ownership was used on a lease basis. Residents of a *demos* could lease a municipal parcel of land upon request. For the Mycenaean Pakijane, the texts in Linear B show a land register (PY Ep 301), in which the parcels, the names and professions of the tenants, the so-called *onateres*, and other peculiarities are recorded (see Ilievski 2000: 83, 155 et seq.); (Fig. 4).

Illustration 4: The oldest cadastral register in Europe with information on municipal land ownership (linear text B from Pylos; PY Ep 301)

Also from the Mycenaean period there are indications of a short-term or long-term rental of usable land for plant cultivation or for livestock farming. Proven as a system, it was established and was valid in various city-states of classical antiquity: "Within the limits of the law, there was room for leasing in various city-states." (see

81

Isager/Skydsgaard 1992: 154). Documents from the Mycenaean period prove that the administrations of the demen paid careful attention to the compliance with procurement conditions. From such a legal document, a clay tablet edited in Linear B; PY Eb 297, it can be deducted that the *demos* of the already mentioned place Pakijane in the city-state of Pylos was concerned with the assignment of a parcel for the priestess Eritha. The priestess awaited the assignment of a kind of official property, but only a piece of land was granted to her for rent (see Schmitt 2010: 18 et seq.).

With increasing population numbers and requests for use, a more differentiated leasing system with corresponding categories and a more detailed description of the land was needed. The detailed terminology is known in particular from the inscriptions of the Attic stelae of the classical era (see Pritchett 1953, 1956):

- *agros* – general term for an agricultural area outside the settlement; field
- *ge psile* - land parcel where cereals, wine, etc., are grown
- *gepedon* - general term for land ownership
- *dryinon* - oak grove
- *kepos* - garden for the cultivation of fruit or vegetables
- *oikopedon* - plot; space for a residential complex
- *orgas* - wooded terrain located on mountain slopes
- *pityinon* - pinewood
- *sukeon* - plantation with fig trees
- *chorion* - land ownership, privately owned land

From the 5th century before common era, Athens demanded property taxes called *eisphora* (see Isager/Skydsgaard 1992: 136), *espherein* meaning bringing in; carrying in; contributing whereby this was exclusively valid in the Athenian state. The historiographer Xenophon called this property tax an instrument of tyranny. This suggests that in the Pre-Mycenaean era, the value of a land parcel leased was measured according to its estimated agricultural yield and the rent was paid as a levy in kind.

Municipal land ownership, which arose in the Old European era, had consequently also been preserved into the Classical Greek era – and, by the way, beyond it. Although the importance of private property increased over time, the leasing system associated with municipal land ownership was widespread in classical antiquity. An example of this is the *demos* of Thorikos, on the southeast coast of the Aegean Sea in the historical landscape of Attica. Founded during the 5th millennium before common era, Thorikos was a *kome*, a village community of Old European affiliation.

Approximately starting from 3,200 before common era, i.e. in the transition phase from Old Europe to the Bronze Age (see Laffineur 2010: 712 et seq.), silver-bearing mines were used in the vicinity of Thorikos, and the silver mining and processing of the metal had its first heyday during Mycenaean times. The silver mines remained in communal ownership at all times. They were administered by the municipal council and the profits were used for the development of the local infrastructure and the quality of life of the community. Foreign investors were able to acquire licenses for the mining of the silver deposits through lease agreements, whereby additional shares of their profits had to be transferred to the municipal

83

council of Thorikos. During the Classical Greek period, Thorikos developed into one of the richest communities in the Athens state (see Bintliff 2012: 270). From an Old European village ti developed to an urban Greek community. Due to its prosperity and its political influence, the place now had the status of a *komopolis*. This is also indicated by the composition of this ancient Greek expression: *kome* in the meaning of settlement from Old European times and *polis* in the meaning of city(state), which is also described as a village state (see Kirsten 1956).

In the late 6th century before common era, Thorikos built its own theatre for its inhabitants and was thus a demen of a total of fourteen owning a theatre. The theatre of Thorikos is one of the oldest in ancient Greece (see Fig. 5). In the course of the 4th century before common era, the space for the audience ranks was expanded, and the theatre could accommodate up to 3,200 visitors.

Illustration 5: model of the theatre of Thorikos (see Roselli 2011: 69)

In Thorikos no building of its own was erected for the Citizens' Council. The representatives of the people held their meetings in the theatre, and in other denominations with theatre they were also used for meetings of the representatives of the citizens. Thorikos became the supra-regional meeting place for the demen of the tribe V.

"Events with more foreigners were suitable for expanding the general level of knowledge. In addition, they served the desirable goal of promoting interaction and solidarity in closely intertwined local networks" (see Ober 2008: 206).

The management of Thorikos in the municipal administration with the primacy of the common good going back to the epoch of Old Europe remained functional throughout all of antiquity until the Middle Ages – with the only interruption in 86 before common era, when the Romans destroyed Thorikos and the place had to be rebuilt.

Even in our epoch, there are examples where municipal councils like the ones elected in Thorikos explicitly administer municipal land ownership with a view to the common good of the population.

In Botswana, southern Africa, the whole country benefits from the yield of silver mines, but especially the cities where those working in the mines live rent-free and where neither school fees nor medical expenses are incurred. And in the capital Gaborone a theater was financed.

In Marinaleda, a village in the south of Spain, all the land is owned and all the property belongs to the municipality, and also the large agricultural cooperative with factory, management, workshops and shop, as well as other facilities of the place, are jointly managed and administrated. All have living space and work, and in addition to a swimming pool, there are green areas and a park and even an amphitheater (see LaBGC and Haarmann, 2019, English translation 2020).

- The new Olympia

At the site of the place of worship of Olympia with the Hera temple, young girls and women gathered already in Old European times to honor the goddess Hera with sporting competitions. The later Olympic Games were created by a diplomatic mission of women, 16 in number, who had managed to negotiate a lasting peace between two warring cities in the Peloponnese. Although Greek democracy only provided for the possibility of ceremonial responsibility in places of worship for all women of the nobility and the wealthy stratum, apparently it had required this special female assignment. As a result, the 16 women were commissioned as a group to organize a festival with competitions in honor of the goddess Hera. This was - so to speak - the beginning of the Olympic Games.

"Every four years, sixteen elderly women weaved a robe for Hera in Olympia (see Pausanias 5.16.2-6; 6.24.10). The origin of this tradition was a committee of elderly women who had at one time been chosen by the sixteen cities of Eleia to settle disputes between the cities of Pisa and Elis. The said elected women, who were considered "the oldest, the most noble and the most valued of all", were very successful in their conciliation and achieved peace for the two cities (see Pausanias 5.16.5). Based on the example of this group, the sixteen women of Elis were commissioned to lead the festival for Hera, which included races for girls and competitions of performances with round dances" (see Connelly 2007: 43).

This assignment was about the promotion of pan-Hellenic togetherness, and it reflects the fundamental values of Old European togetherness, in terms of content and space. The cult site of Olympia with the temple of Hera, has not been used by the Greeks for sports games. The pre-Greek name for competition, *amilla,* also indicates the connection to Old Europe. In ancient Greek, there are two terms with different meanings: rivalry, competition. One is *amilla* with the connotation of peaceful competition, the other is *eris* as competition, conflict, and military confrontation.

The traditional historiography has largely obscured the mission of the 16 women and their role in Greek antiquity, which still shapes European historiography today. In our history books, the origin of the Olympic competition is attributed to male initiative. It is only true that men created the legitimation myth that Heracles had set up the Olympic Games in honor of Zeus and usurped the holy place Olympia with this "legitimation". The men took over the stadium and also attributed its planning to Heracles. The construction of the temple of Zeus began during the 8th century before common era was then completed in 456 before common era. Hera and the heritage of Old Europe in Olympia was no longer mentioned. The same was the case for the Olympic competition of women. The Olympics had become another signal of male-centered rule. After all, the basic idea of a peaceful competition remained, even though the Olympic Games were now held in honor of Zeus and no longer in honor of Hera.

The first Olympic Games of modern times took place in Athens in 1896 without women participating in the competition.

"Apparently, the main braking effect was the founder of the Games, Baron Pierre de Coubertin: He was a great opponent of the admission of women to the competitions. Apparently, he never changed this opinion: When women already participated in the games, he still emphasized in the 1930s that male performance should prove itself at the Olympic Games." (see Tzshoppe 2016).

Four years later, at the Olympic Games in Paris, women participated once again for the first time in the sports of golf and tennis. What followed was the admission to figure skating and swimming and in 1928 to gymnastics and athletics. However, the majority of the organizers of the games are still men, men with an agenda, oriented towards financial interests related to geopolitical power struggles and power protests. The fact that the games were originally the celebration of the common responsibility for the preservation of what was due to a power above man and a unity in the togetherness was forgotten or hidden with phrases.

- **Festivals and rituals**

Like the playful competition in Olympia, all other festivals were first and foremost dedicated to the honor of the deities. The festivities of antiquity began with processions which were led by priestesses. The fact that the processions were largely determined by pre-Greek

89

traditions is shown by the core term "procession" *thiasos*, an expression of Old European origin. These parades were an essential part of the communication between man and deity, and at the same time they were rituals for communal cohesion.

"The processions offered a particularly visible and dramatic display in which the leaders and participants well understood their role. Their movements were a reflection of the structures and values of the community. The women who led these processions walked together in the spotlight which underlined their activity and symbolic prestige in the multitude of believers" (see Connelly 2007: 167).

The processions were firmly anchored in the calendar of municipal festivities. The exact point in time of a festivity cannot be indicated by date, because in the Athens state two calendars, one civil and one ritual calendar, were in use, and this was the orientation of all regions of Greece. The civil calendar was made of ten months based on the changing presidency of the Prytania of the ten tribes. Twelve months were distinguished in the ritual calendar. This is the reason why the coordination of religious festivals on the one hand and public events on the other was not easy at all (see Ober 2008: 195).

In addition to the spiritual meaning, rulers used the processions to demonstrate to the public the importance and influence of a state-sponsored cult. Whether in honor of the goddess Athena, other goddesses or male gods such as Dionysus, the Athenian state or one of the other city states or a city alone presented themselves with the procession as guardians of the right order. In addition to the compliance with the religious ritual traditions, this also included the observance of the demen order.

There were festivals reserved exclusively for men, for example, fraternity festivals, phrases, and women-only festivals, for example, the Skira in May/June (see Ober 2008: 195).

The largest women's festival in the Greek ritual calendar was the Thesmophoria held in September/October. The first day was *anodos,* which means the way up. The married women of whatever status came together and climbed up to Thesmophorion, the sacred meeting place for this feast. The priests of the pre-Greek Demeter recounted the myth of the Demeter and told stories about this goddess. On the second day, *nesteia,* fasting, only the consumption of the seeds of the pomegranate was allowed. Seeds that fell to the ground were meant for the dead. On the third day, Demeter was celebrated as *Kalligeneia,* the goddess of happy birth.

Demeter's great festival of Thesmophoria, celebrated throughout the Greek world, was only addressed to married women. It was organized and carried out by a hierarchy of women who left their homes and their husbands for the duration of the feast. During the first half of the 2nd century before common era, Satyra, a priestess of Thesmophoria, was honored by her native *demos*, Milete, for having faithfully and devotedly performed her obligations for sacrificial acts and for her charity to restore the sanctuaries of Demeter and Plouton" (see Connelly 2007: 42).

The name of the festival is derived from the pre-Greek *thesmos* and means statute. The name refers to the divine laws which oblige people to cultivate and preserve the land. These laws, as well as the ritual festival itself, give the impression of "extraordinary

91

antiquity" (see Burkert 1985: 13) and are indeed ancient in the sense of very old, namely from the era of Old Europe. This also applies to the following custom, which was one of the main ritual acts of Old European origin. The half-decomposed parts of piglets which had been cut up last year and thrown into sacrificial pits were placed on altars, then mixed with seeds and, accompanied by prayers, they were finally incorporated into the soil. This fertility ritual should encourage a rich harvest. From the epoch of Old Europe, this ritual had apparently also reached Lithuania, where it is described in a script of the 18th century after our time (see Gimbutas 1996, 229). Clay figures of piglets with pressed-in wheat grains from the 5th millennium before common era also prove the origin of the Greek Thesmophoria from the era of Old Europe.

The processions and rituals with which Athena, the supreme goddess in the Athenian state cult, was celebrated, were spread throughout the year. They started in spring with the procession, in which young able-bodied men from a temple on the Acropolis, which existed before the Parthenon, carried a heavy statue of Athena made of solid wood several miles to the coast, where women cleaned it with the saline seawater.

During the months of June and July, respectively, the most important of the festivals associated with Athena, the multi-day Panathenaia, followed. Its program was extensive: ritual prayers led by priestesses in thanksgiving for the harvest – the Panathenaia were at the same time the Thanksgiving of the Athenians – chants in which the birth of Athena was sung and the performance of the Pyrrhic dance, which myths report Athena danced for the first time after her victory over the giants. In the myths, Panathenaia is still called

Athenaia, and it is reported that the festival was held for the first time more than seven centuries before the Greek Olympic games. This would refer to the Mycenaean era (during the 15th or 14th century BCE). During the 6th century before common era, the tyrant Peisistratos is said to have equipped the festival particularly lavishly with musical and sporting competitions, and from inscriptions going back to the 4th century before common era it appears that there was even a horse race in addition to other competitions on the occasion of the Great Panathenaia.

In this context, a distinction was made between two variants of the festival. The *mikra,* so the little Panathenaia was committed every year. The *megala*, the great Panathenaia, took place every four years and had a special program item: With every great Panathenaia, the huge statue of Athena in the Parthenon was given a new robe (see Burkert 1985: 141). The new garment was worn in a solemn procession into the Parthenon, where a priestess and her assistants, all young women from aristocratic families, took off the old garment from the statue and put on the new one. This ritual act is depicted in the picture frieze of the temple (see Lagerlöf 2000: 120 et seq.).

The Chalkeia Festival was held in autumn. Under the supervision of a priest, an oversized loom was built on which selected aristocratic girls worked on the new robe for the huge statue of Athena in the Parthenon in the basic colors purple and yellow and weaved scenes of mythical history, such as the victory of Athena over the giant Enkelados and the victory of the Olympians over the other giants (see Gantz 1993: 448 et seq.). Working time and rhythm of work were chosen so that the ritual garment for the goddess was completed every four years for the Great Panathenaia Festival.

The custom of dressing the goddess Athena in a new robe every four years was preserved over all crises of the so-called Athenian democracy. It even survived the Macedonian royal period. Even doubts about the truthfulness of the myth of the victory of the Olympians over the giants and other myths during the age of Pericles did not change the Athenian state cult. None of the critical attitudes to the old myths "seem to have interrupted the religion of the *polis*. On the contrary, their strengths and weaknesses manifest themselves in conceptual flexibility, which is subject to careful observance of rites and rituals of the cult" (see Lagerlöf 2000: 135). The value of traditionally recurring festivals for self-understanding and cohesion within a society was known to the organizers and was maintained accordingly.

To this day, some traditions, with functional transformation from polytheistic cult to Marian cult, have been preserved in Greece. Thus, the procession in honor of the Old European goddess of agriculture, Demeter, on the *hieros dromos*, the holy road from Athens to Eleusis – celebrated in ancient Greece in July/ August and framed by the Eleusinian mysteries – is still held, with this sacred performance nowadays dedicated to the Virgin Mary, who took the place of the Old European mother of grain Demeter (see Gable 1990: 34 et seq.). And the Panathenaia were also so significant in the spiritual-cultural life of the people that the main day of the Great Panathenaia, August 13, was further traded over the centuries and finally found its place in the Christian feast calendar as the Assumption of the Virgin Mary – especially celebrated by the Mediterranean coastal communities in many places for three days with a rich program for the population. In Scandinavia, the midsummer festivals reflect this tradition.

- The spiritual superstructure

In Ancient Greece, there were already city-states and thus borders with other city-states, but there were no religions yet. The numerous Greek deities can only be found in the spirituality of the people. The narratives of the myths describe the manifold interconnections and entanglements assigning their respective place to the gods and goddesses. Let us confine ourselves to the contemplation of pre-Greek deities who occupied a central position and gave guidance to the Greek population.

"Start at the hearth fire" was said in ancient times and meant to ensure good success. The saying stands for the spiritually shaped way of thinking of the time when all action was under the aegis of the deities. In every house, the hearth *hestia* was the place for the indispensable daily rituals for the goddess with the same name, Hestia. According to archaeological and literary sources, before eating, it was customary to pour potions on the hearth fire and throw a small portion of the food on it as an offering for Hestia (see Nilsson 1967: 337 et seq.).

The goddess Themis watched over the observance of traditional and spiritual norms in everyday life in Greek society. Themis was considered a personification of consistency and tradition. The expression *themis esti* which literally means "it is custom" describes the fundamental importance of the conventions cultivated over many generations in dealing with each other and in traditional values, and the noun *themis* stands for righteousness, traditional customs and traditions, social norm, the right political order. In Homer's works and in other sources of epic literature, the terms are used within this meaning. As a goddess with her own cult, Themis has been worshipped since the classical era in Thessaly, Boetia, Epiros, the Argolis, Macedonia and Rhodes (see Stafford 1997: 158 et seq.). As a goddess of permanence and tradition, Themis is directly associated with the demen order and not with the exclusive privileges of the elitist power.

The rural areas with the demen were under the protection of Artemis, the goddess of the untouched nature, as well as the populated and formed landscape, which is expressed in the name Artemis *demosynos* : "Artemis, patron of the lands of the demen" (see Beekes 2010: 325).

Demeter blessed the fertility of the plants. The name of the goddess is composed of *de* for earth and *meter* for mother.

Athena was the icon of the state order. She was the patron of the citizens of the city-state and its institutions. Symbolically, Athena was associated with the People's Assembly (*ekklesia*), the People's Court(*heliaia*) and the Areopagus, the oldest institution in Athens. According to the myths the Greeks imagined that Athena had set up the People's Assembly and led it, so to speak, as a mythical chairwoman. In his tragedy *Eumenides,* the well-meaning Goddesses, in the third part of the work *Oresteia* written in 458 before common era Aeschylus alludes to this (see Bremmer/Erskine 2010: 189 et seq.).

In ancient times, Hestia and Themis were considered deities of the "second" generation, that is, daughters of the primordial deities

Gaia, earth, and Uranus, heaven; (*see Theogony* 132-38). The orientation of the Greeks towards these goddesses implied the awareness according to which the social conventions of the community building were not man-made, but divinely inspired.

6.   Democracy criticism by Plato and Aristotle

What was the meaning of democracy in ancient times? For the critics, the state that Cleisthenes had reached with his reforms and the supposed democracy was synonymous with the despotic rule of the poor over the rich. Of the intellectuals and contemporary witnesses of that epoch, only a few have embedded the new form of government in an overall perspective of alternatives to rule, such as Plato and Aristotle. The two philosophers give an insight into their thoughts on *demokratia* and are indicators of the assessment of the supposed first democracy.

-   Plato

Plato's reflections are outstanding in his works *Politeia*, Republic, written around 380 before common era, *Politikos*, Statesman, written between 365 and 347 before common era, and *Nomoi*, The Laws, written as a late work around 360 before common era. Plato puts the various possible forms of rule into a spiral with a descending trend of development (see Cahn 2002): aristocracy, timocracy, oligarchy, democracy, tyranny.

Aristocracy as the "rule of the best" is Plato's only favorite form from his enumeration. He idealizes the rule of the best as a model for a just state order.

This concept has often been misinterpreted, for Plato did not want to see nobles at the head of the responsibility for a state. The explanation lies in the composition of the word: *aristos,* excellent, magnificent, and *kratia,* dominion. In his political utopia, Plato developed ideas

99

for a state having ideal administrative structures and an ideal social order in the Dialogue *Politeia* in which he describes the executives or public servants as aristocrats. But not as those who are born into their status and represent their elitist interests. Plato's ideal image of an aristocrat is based on the fundamental meaning of the attribute *aristos*: noble, best, finest, most gifted, most virtuous, most exemplary. This attribute refers to "noble" qualities, namely special abilities and talents, the skill in dealing with municipal affairs, as well as the foresight. For this reason, in the sense of Plato aristocracy means the leadership of a state by leaders with having special gifts. This form corresponds most closely to the Old European understanding of authority as a selection criterion for the assumption of responsibility.

Plato's aristocrats are elected because of their abilities, and it makes no difference whether they come from wealthy families, are of noble descent, or come from low-income social classes. In his ideal conception, those who are suitable for a candidacy for the office of an aristocrat complete a comprehensive training in administration, social teaching and life experience as well as an intensive philosophical training. They must refrain from the accumulation of personal wealth and devote themselves entirely to the promotion of the common good and the maintenance of the just order whereby this is based on the worship of the gods. This is expressly stated in Book III of the *Politeia* and means the veneration of creation and the obligation of responsibility for its preservation.

So what distinguishes law enforcement in the sense of Plato is the authority granted to the aristocrats on the basis of their suitability and confirmed within the framework of a selection. In this context, what is crucial is the egalitarian principle of choice and not the assumption of official powers as a result of the exercise of power. And completely contrary to the social norms of his time, Plato's state model sees men and women equally in leadership positions, for which all suitable persons are to be comprehensively trained.

Plato did not comment on the size of the body of law enforcement officials. In his model of the body, cooperative action and renunciation are decisive monopolies of power. In Plato's state model, a monopoly of power has not described the supreme official as a "philosopher-king" – man or woman.

In the history of modern philosophy, the term philosopher-king has been mistaken for the figure of an actual king. Plato, however, describes the philosopher-king in the chairmanship of the lawmen/lawwomen as a person having an exemplary character. Whoever is elected to this position has undergone as rigorous training and aptitude tests as the other law enforcement officers. Furthermore, a "golden soul" is expected from the person in the presidency, which means that this person should be the most righteous of all. Plato's understanding of aristocracy as a special aptitude correlates with the levelness of the Old European affiliation, which was precisely based on entrusting the responsibility for the community to particularly capable persons by choice.

Plato's model of the state administration under the supervision of law enforcement as an "aristocracy" could be understood as a model of the model realized within the framework of the institutions of the European Union, the European technocracy. The role of Plato's king philosopher could be compared to the legendary role of King Arthur in the circle of his knights. The introduction of the Round Table as a forum for discussions and deliberations assigned the same position to all participants (see Castleden 2000). The position of the king, the chairman of the round, was not elevated. This means that there was neither a throne nor an elevated pedestal to mark his status.

After the aristocracy, in Plato's downward spiral the state models of timocracy, oligarchy, democracy and tyranny remain, all of which are criticized and rejected by Plato.

Timocracy, the rule of those who strive for honor and glory (*time,* honor; value + *kratia*) is, according to Plato's argument, a degeneration of the aristocracy in such a manner that in the next generation there are no longer fully represented intellectual and moral virtues, but the pursuit of fame, then satisfied by wars with neighboring states. This situation would weaken the state by diverting it fro its real task of promoting the well-being of the population and increasing the well-being of all. In such an environment, the order would further degenerate by bringing forth the next weaker stage:

Oligarchy, rule of the few over others (*oligos,* few + *archein,* conduct, lead) leads for Plato to the irreconcilable contrast existing between a rich upper class and the mass of poor people. Oligarchs no longer espouse any social ideals and virtues like the aristocrats but are only interested in increasing their own wealth and in exploiting the people dominated by them. The political power and responsibility for the destinies of the population lie exclusively in the hands of a few rich people. At the same time, material wealth is the exclusive key to admission to the circle of the elite. This isolation of the wealthy elite from the majority of the population results in unbearable tensions, which inevitably lead to an uprising of the ownerless masses.

Democracy as the rule of the common people (*demos* + *kratia* in Plato's model, has passed from the oligarch to his son, the "democratic man". His political power distracts him from what really counts in life. He develops unnecessary desires, despises the customary law and the teachings of parents and ancestors in favor of a selfish pursuit of more power and influence. Moderation in behavior is as foreign to the "democratic man" as respect for the wisdom of those having a better education than him. Sooner or later, the democratic rule would result in the dissolution of order and society becoming chaotic and ungovernable.

Plato's rejection of the model of democracy is due to the dramatic events in connection with the trial of his mentor Socrates, who was accused of "ungodliness" (asebeia) (see Haarmann 2019: 28 et seq.), and justifies his suicide.

Allegedly, Socrates had neglected the worship of the deities of Athens and instead propagated "foreign" gods, namely those of the arch-enemy Sparta. The charge was treason and deception of the Athenian youth (see Waterfield 2009). Socrates' advocacy of pantheism and his conciliar attitude toward Sparta led to prejudice by the members of the political leadership, for they saw "… how his appearance, his conduct, and his challenge to public order tested the limits of the ideals of openness and freedom of expression propagated by Athenian democrats" (see Hall 2014: 152). A defamation scheme led to the indictment in 399 before common era. Finally, the panel of jurors declared Socrates guilty by 280 votes to 220 and, in a second vote, set the death penalty.

Socrates renounced the possibility of requesting the conversion of the sentence into an exile, by explaining to his followers that he would rather die than leave his beloved Athens. In addition, he was at such an old age that he would not survive the years of exile anyway. So he chose suicide through the poison cup.

The condemnation of his mentor has exposed Plato as a machination of schemers against a highly intelligent and honest critic. The traumatic experience of the show trial against Socrates led Plato to brand the contemporary democracy with its demagogues and manipulators. This was resented by posterity, especially in the democratically minded modern era, and has motivated the predominantly negative attitude towards Platonism among many Platonists of the modern age (see Reinhard 2012).

Tyranny, the form of government of the sole ruler (*tyrannos,* tyrant), plunges society into chaos because of the lack of discipline and because of the disproportionate behavior of the "democratic men", and this hopeless situation calls a strong man on the plan, the tyrant. According to Plato, this is the worst of all rulers. He usurps power within the state, creates a deceptive order according to his ideas and conditions for the unilateral promotion of his selfish interests, without considering the consequences of his actions for society. The laws are practically repealed. The ruled hated the autocrat, but were powerless against him. Because of his lawlessness, however, the tyrant lived a life like in a prison created by himself. The only prospect that remains is hopelessness.

Plato explains the essence of responsible politics in his dialogue "Statesman", *Politikos*. In this dialogue, Plato develops ideal conceptions of a leadership of the state caring about the well-being of all and representing the interests of the state. The responsible people were distinguished by specialized knowledge, *gnosis*, which enabled them to manage the state business. Plato tries to differentiate the role of the politician from that of the philosopher. Essentially, for Plato the matter is the responsibility that many rulers lack. This idea is formulated by Plato in his dialogue "The Stranger" (*xenos*).

In his work *Nomoi*, the last of Plato's dialogues, Plato asks who deserves the honor of recording laws which are capable of maintaining a political order. This is more important than the question: What is law? Plato's arguments about the laws do not refer to conceptualizations of what is called positive law in legal history, that is, a collection of laws whose provisions are valid regardless of religious beliefs. Plato's conception of law is shaped by the contemporary notion of a divinely inspired customary law, the realization of which included the observance of ritual acts with which the gods are honored (see Lutz 2012). Since divinely inspired, the customary law should not be changed, because every change carries the germ of an abuse by the rulers.

- **Aristotle**

For Aristotle, democracy was the rule of the needy, the so-called *aporoi* who just thought of the satisfaction of their needs. In his work "Politics" *Politika*, Aristotle states that the ideal rule must be in the hands of wealthy aristocrats. They would have the time and leisure to take care of the affairs of the state and would not be under pressure to earn their livelihoods, which would burden the less wealthy (see Martin et al. 2003).

For Aristotle, democracy is the perversion of a constitutional form of rule (Fig. 6).

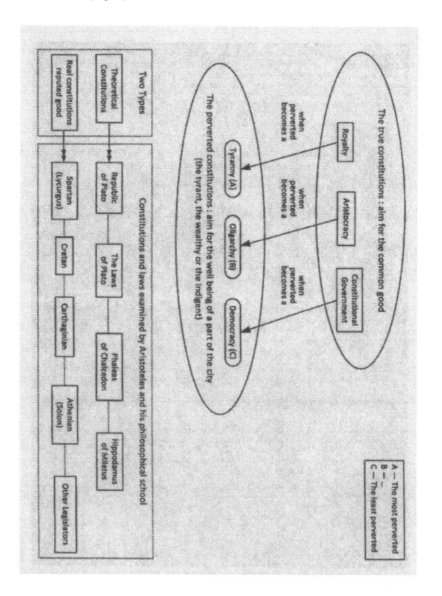

Illustration 6: Conceptualization and categorization of forms of
domination in the work *Politika* by Aristotle (see Book III, chap. 7-14;
Book IV, chap. 4-10)

For Aristotle, the most important role of a politician is that of a legislator, *nomothetes*. If the order in the state of the city-state is ensured by laws, the politician has the task of monitoring the compliance with the laws. Aristotle compares the activity of the politician with that of a craftsman, *demiourgos*, such as a weaver or shipbuilder. The politician is someone who uses his practical knowledge to create something concrete out of it. For Aristotle one point is pretty clear: The politician creates laws, while the shipbuilder creates watercraft (see Simpson 1998). Aristotle does not ask the question of social relevance and political consequences.

In his *Politika*, Aristotle makes some strikingly sarcastic remarks about the nature of democracy. For example, he advocates the granting of voting rights to craftsmen, but warns that elections should not be held too frequently and reflects on the way craftsmen, who would be elected as representatives of their demen to the People's Assembly (*ekklesia*), participate in political decision-making processes. Craftsmen were employed from early to late in their workshops. So they could not spare much time for meetings of the People's Assembly. Their workload will prevent them from attending frequently held meetings. This would increase the likelihood that the aristocrats would remain among themselves in the People's Assembly.

Aristotle was also completely unimpressed by his mentor Plato's attitude towards women. Aristotle represented the chauvinist social model of his contemporaries. He considered women to be less intelligent than men, and he did not trust them with organizational talent or leadership skills. For Aristotle, the transfer of responsibility for state affairs to women was completely out of the question.

7.   Hope and motivation

The European Union has been consolidated in an era of untroubled political perspectives, and the fundamental values have been written on the flags of faith in progress. These were the 1990s, when the whole world gave itself the illusion that the Cold War was irrevocably over and that the understanding of democracy would now also take root in the former socialist states, and that the EU could be enlarged indefinitely. The illusions are shattered in the storm of events.

The assumption that democratic principles can be transplanted all over the world has also crumbled more and more in the course of the recent years. Our understanding of democracy is weak and our willingness to act in solidarity and implement a sustainable crisis management, wherever in the world, is by no means free of our own interests. This had and still has consequences. Refugee flows and misery on all continents, triggered by rising sea levels, drought, lack of drinking water and food, by struggles for the "right" religion and belief in the "right" God, by wars for land and power – the most terrible scenarios, shocking fates, unbearable hardship.

So what to do now?

"Since we do not know what the future will bring, the experiences of the past are the only basis for the building of our knowledge," wrote Immanuel Kant in his *Critique of Pure Reason* (see its first edition of 1781, and its 2nd heavily modified edition of 1787). Kant's formulation is an expression of his positive basic attitude towards remembering, namely the willingness to learn from history and to give meaning to one's own actions in the world.

In this context, the anthropologist Oliver Kozlarek affirms: "Sense generation is important for all people. It is one of the conditions to live a fulfilling and dignified life. In other words, the lack of meaning is dehumanizing. The meaning generation is a core aspect of building the world" (see Kozlarek et al. 2012a: 9).

The question is now: How can we still recognize a meaning when crises and wars destroy personal livelihoods as well as the trust in the world's leaders?

The meaning generation arises within one's own radius of action. It lies in our inner drive, from which we do something, so to say in an intrinsic motivation. We want to help, we want to do well, we want to repeat what we do well, we want to do it better, improve it, create something new that benefits ourselves as well as others. We enjoy the pride that we feel when something succeeds, and the recognition that we receive for our commitment, for our work. This pride becomes an extrinsic motivation by strengthening our further action.

And it was precisely this *condition humaine*that resulted in the construction of the high culture of Old Europe. There was consensus on rights and duties, which had developed mythoculturally in the experience that each individual is important for the functioning of the whole and that this whole is surrounded by an extraordinary force. Consequently, the culmination plateau of this primordial democracy which has not yet been realized in full bloom anywhere else after Old Europe could emerge. How, we can realize it, if we activate our cultural memory, stimulation and impulse.

From our point of view there is another fundamental aspect concerning the manners, because they mark the form of dialogues and cooperation. We don't like it at all when other people behave towards us in a derogatory or encroaching manner, even aggressively or even just arrogantly lecturing or ignorant. And when we consciously listen and watch ourselves, we find ourselves speaking and acting in the same manner. The reflection on your own actions and your own way of speaking can help you adjust.

To gain this conclusion, it is not even necessary to have read Kant who affirmed: "Act only in accordance with that maxim through which you can at the same time will that it become a universal law" (*Critique of Practical Reason*, Section 7 "Basic Law of Pure Practical Reason", p. 54). Nor must one have recognized his categorical imperative as an elementary principle of ethics in the different variants included in his works *Fundamentals of the Metaphysics of Morals* (1785) and *Critique of Practical Reason* (1788). However, it clearly confirms that a socially responsible action is based on treating other people the way one expects to be treated by others.

Beyond one's own radius of action, it is difficult to recognize Kant's postulate of the equivalence of rights and duties in the world. If we look at an emblematic event of the same epoch, the French Revolution of 1789, the ideals *liberté, égalité, fraternité* make us stubborn. Other than the term equality suggests it was not at all about the equality of all people and certainly not about the equality of the sexes. The term fraternity reveals it. The concept of freedom also remained a lip service of the revolutionaries at the time and was intended too briefly. The same can be said about the idea of the freedom of the individual and his equality before the law, which was made an icon in the American Declaration of Independence in 1776. Neither of these was intended for slaves. The indigenous population, the Old Americans – still called *Indians* by the expression of traditional ignorance – was not even mentioned. But at least: The cultural memory had been loudly reported and gave food for thought.

Were there such impulses for social and economic issues? In 1776, Adam Smith's work The Wealth of Nations was published and became dramatically emblematic. Smith relied on the self-regulation of the markets and has probably not been able to see the devastating effect, so the winner of the Nobel Prize in Economics 2016, the Finnish Bengt Holmström. Smith's work became the cornerstone of predatory capitalism, and it was not until 1859 that someone publicly opposed it: Karl Marx. First with his "Critique of Political Economy" and in 1867 with the first volume of his three-part work "Capital". In the course of the twentieth century, especially due to the disastrous consequences of the first world economic crisis, this renewed thought impetus from the depths of cultural memory intensified the efforts to create a social market economy in the true sense. However, since then this social market economy has been and is currently more or less threatened by powerful strippers.

The existence of the societies of Old Europe and the actions of the people there prove that a balanced coexistence was a reality. *Amilla*, the peaceful competition, and *kairos*, the right moment, the right measure, balance, thoughtful action, profit as a result of thoughtful action, were the components of *eirene*, peace in the sense

112

of a state of peaceful living conditions. All three terms are of Old European origin and still exist in the Greek language today.

"From 6000 to 3000 before common era, this linchpin of the Old European political thought was not a utopia, but a self-evident political reality from which normativity emerged, despite all its inadequate implementation. In the face of world problems that unite humanity which is at least united from a technological, informational and economic point of view, the differentiated unity gains a radically new explosiveness and topicality. And together with it, a second Old European central motif becomes newly effective: the connection between polis and the world, the original scene of a cosmopolitanism which still echoes in Kant's vision of eternal peace, when he states that a guarantee of eternal peace and an obligation to it is that the different members of the human family are allowed to live and should live everywhere. Exchange, cultivation of hospitality law, independence and connection of the different cultures is almost a moral imperative of coexistence.
What's more, this is the foundation of a reasonable world bourgeoisie in times of danger" (Seubert 2019).

If we become aware that the fundamental values that we no longer think about because we take them for granted have long, long ago been understood as essential, and if we realize that the potential to implement fundamental values in society is not only anchored in our cultural memory, but also available as a *condition humaine*, then this fact should motivate us to activate the potential for the generation of the upcoming changes. The immense distortions in all areas of the present advanced civilizations make this necessity absolutely clear.

So let's be hopeful:

"All truly radical, time-renewing currents take a while to leave the stages of the collective unconscious and preconscious and truly begin to change the consciousness and the being of society" (see Hinrichs 2018: 19).

The refreshing of the cultural memory and finally the update of outdated historiography and its diffusion across media by means of words and images may speed up the process.

Epilogue: Scipio Africanus' Dream

Finally, let's move on to a vision:

In his work written in 54 before common era and entitled *On the State*, Cicero, by using the fictitious story of a dream, introduces his beliefs a good citizen should be guided by. For this purpose, he lets Scipio Africanus, general and statesman of the Roman Republic, tell a dream.

The dream lies behind two decades. In this dream, his grandfather, Scipio Africanus the Elder, appeared to him among others and sent him on a journey through time in which he showed him his future tasks and life stages. His grandfather had also shown him how tiny the earth was in the circle of planets and that the Roman Empire was just a little point and how small the human being was as well and how deaf the human being had become to the cosmic sounds. He had let him know that earthly fame was worthless and eternal fame was impossible because both would perish with death anyway. On the other hand, what remains for the eternity is what is constantly moving out of itself while what has to be driven from the outside, is soulless. His grandfather, he said, had admonished him for justice and had explained to him that only after many years of lonely circles outside the earth an evildoer could return to a place in heaven. The reference to the division of the earth into climate zones was also important to the grandfather.

For Cicero, it was a matter of responsibility. The task of "the human being subjugating nature" was as unthinkable to him as monotheism was. And so he posits that the blunting of the connection to the Divine as the superordinate force leads to putting personal interests at the center of one's own doing and pursuits. Furthermore, Cicero, like Plato, revered by him, thought that besides the responsibility for creation the fundamental rights and duties were the foundation without which there cannot be any prosperous existence of the community. Cicero's fiction of Scipio's dream can be interpreted as an appeal to remain attentive and agile to a perpetual mobile, to understand oneself as a small part of a large whole, and to act in a responsibly and just manner.

The roots of community building with all stabilizing values lie within us, deep in our subconscious. Let us let the knowledge grow from our cultural memory and let us ensure that memory does not remain in mere repetition of concepts and is a filler for Sunday speeches, as quickly forgotten as facts learned for an examination, which, once queried, are already superimposed. Instead, we should value history as something that makes visible paths that others have already gone before us. Furthermore, we should evaluate which paths led to peaceful togetherness and prosperity and when and for which reason which obstacles blocked this path.

Wars, crises, short periods of peace. Why is it so difficult to bring the experience of human history, crystallized in more than 3000 continuous peaceful years in Old Europe, to the screen of our memory? Just because the canon of our school education presents classical Greece as the cradle of our Western basic values and the pre-Greek history is still hidden? In this regard, the British writer and political commentator Sir Robert Ferdinand Mount who is fan of classical models states:

"We have adopted some high principles of Athens and Rome: tolerance, and awareness as responsible citizens, and equality and democracy. And we picked up on some pleasant habits. But somehow Scipio's dream got lost. And the search teams are still on their way to track him down" (see Mount 2010: 378).

A long time ago, however, Scipio Africanus' dream was already a reality. So, we've already had what we absolutely need to remember today: legitimate trust in the work of those who run our communities, wherever they are, as long as they do it in full awareness of the basic values – for the good of ALL of us.

Bibliography

Acemoglu, Daron / Robinson, James A. (2012). Why nations fail. The origins of power, prosperity and poverty. Profile Books

Albertz, Rainer / Hiesel, Gerhard / Klengel, Horst / Koch, Heidemarie /
Niemeyer, Hans Georg / Wiesehöfer, Josef / Zibelius-

Chen, Karola (2003). Frühe Hochkulturen. Ägypter - Sumerer - Assyrer
- Babylonier - Hethiter - Minoer - Phöniker - Perser. Stuttgart: Theiss (2nd ed.)

Allen, Nicholas J. / Callan, Hilary / Dunbar, Robin / James, Wendy (eds.) (2011). Early human kinship. From sex to social reproduction.
Malden, MA & Oxford: Wiley-Blackwell

Anthony, David W. (2009). The rise and fall of Old Europe, in: Anthony
/ Chi 2009: 28-57

Anthony, David W. / Chi, Jennifer Y. (eds.) (2009). The lost world of
Old Europe - The Danube valley, 5000 - 3500 BC. Princeton, NJ &
Oxford: Princeton University Press

Assmann, Aleida (2018a). Menschenrechte und Menschenpflichten. Schlüsselbegriffe für eine humane Gesellschaft. Vienna: Picus Verlag - (2018b). Der europäische Traum. Vier Lehren aus der Geschichte.
Munich: C.H. Beck (2nd ed.)

Badiou, Alain (2012). Plato's *Republic*. A dialogue in 16 chapters (translated by Susan Spitzer and Introduction by Kenneth Reinhard). New
York: Columbia University Press

Barber, Benjamin R. (2013). If mayors ruled the world. Dysfunctional nations, rising cities. New Haven, Connecticut: Yale University Press

Bailey, Geoff / Spikins, Penny (eds.) (2008). Mesolithic Europe. Cambridge and New York: Cambridge University Press

Beekes, Robert (2010). Etymological dictionary of Greek, 2 vols. Leiden & Boston: Brill

Bem, Catalin (2007). Traian-Dealul Fântânilor. Fenomenul Cucuteni AB. Bucharest: Muzeul National de Istorie a României

Bintliff, John (2012). The complete archaeology of Greece. From hunter-gatherers to the 20th century A.D. Malden, MA & Oxford:
Wiley-Blackwell

Blackwell, C.W. (ed.) (2003). Demos: Classical Athenian democracy (A. Mahoney / R. Scaife, eds. The Stoa. a consortium for scholarly publication in the humanities [www.stoa.org])

Blok, Josine / Lardinois, André (eds.) (2006). Solon: New historical and philological perspectives. Leiden: E.J. Brill

Boardman, John / Griffin, Jasper / Murray, Oswyn (eds.) (1986). Greece and the Hellenistic world. Oxford & New York: Oxford University Press

Bolmarcich, Sarah (2010). Demes, in: Gagarin / Fantham 2010: 390

Bregman, Rudger (2017). Utopia for Realists. London: Bloomsbury
Publishing

Bremmer, Jan N. / Erskine, Andrew (eds.) (2010). The gods of ancient Greece. Identities and transformations. Edinburgh: Edinburgh University Press

Cahn, Steven M. (2002). Classics of political and moral philosophy. Oxford & New York: Oxford University Press

Cartledge, Paul Anthony (2016). Democracy: A life. Oxford: Oxford
University Press

Castleden, Rodney (2000). King Arthur. The truth behind the legend.
London & New York: Routledge

Cermáková, E. (2007). Die Stellung der Frau, des Mannes und des Kindes in der Gesellschaft der Begründer der Lengyel-Kultur, in: Kazdová /
Podborsky 2007: 207-255

Chantraine, Pierre (2009). Dictionnaire étymologique de la langue grecque. Histoire des mots. Paris: Klinksieck (2nd ed.)

Chapman, John (2000). Fragmentation in archaeology: People, places and broken objects in the prehistory of South-Eastern Europe. London
& New York: Routledge

- (2009). Houses, households, villages, and proto-cities in southeastern
Europe, in: Anthony / Chi 2009: 75-89

Cintas-Peña, Marta. In: Simon, Raúl. Una investigación bucea hasta el Neolítico para encontrar los orígines de la desigualdad entre hombres y mujeres. In: El País 15.04.2021

Cline, Eric H. (ed.) (2010). The Oxford handbook of the Bronze Age
Aegean. Oxford & New York: Oxford University Press

Comsa, E. / Cantacuzino, G. (2001). Necropola neolitica de la Cernica.
Bucharest

Connelly, Joan Breton (2007). Portrait of a priestess. Women and ritual in ancient Greece. Princeton, NJ & Oxford: Princeton University Press

Curta, Florin (ed.) (2010). Neglected Barbarians. Turnhout: Brepols

Curtis, D.A. (ed.) (1996). Cleisthenes the Athenian. An essay on the representation of space and time in Greek political thought from the end of the sixth century to the death of Plato. Atlantic-Highlands, NJ: Humanities

Dahl, Robert Alan (1989). Democracy and its critics. New Haven: Yale University Press

Dashu, Max (2005). Knocking down straw dolls, in: Feminist Theology 13: 185-216

Deger-Jalkotzy, Sigrid (1991). Diskontinuität und Kontinuität: Aspekte politischer und sozialer Organisation in mykenischer Zeit und in der Welt der Homerischen Epen, in: Musti et al. 1991: 53-66

Dement'eva, Vera V. / Schmitt, Tassilo (eds.) (2010). Volk und Demokratie im Altertum. Göttingen: Edition Ruprecht

Dickinson, Oliver (1994). The Aegean Bronze Age. Cambridge & New York: Cambridge University Press

Donlan, Walter (1997). The relations of power in the pre-state and early state polities, in: Mitchell / Rhodes 1997: 39-48

Dümling, Sebastian, AfD (um 1500), in: Merkur 31 October 2018

Dunbar, Robin (1993). Coevolution of neocortex size, group size and language in humans, in: Behavioral Brain Science 16: 681-735 Düring, Ingemar (2005). Aristoteles. Darstellung und Interpretation seines Denkens. Heidelberg: Winter (2nd ed.)

Earle, Timothy (1997). How chiefs come to power. The
political economy in prehistory. Stanford: Stanford University
Press

Fokken, Ulrike (2013). Ort der Gerechten – Die rote Insel. In:
taz,
16.02.2013

Foxhall, Lin (1997). A view from the top: Evaluating the
Solonian property classes, in: Mitchell / Rhodes 1997: 113-136

Gagarin, Michael/Fantham, Elaine (eds.) (2010). The Oxford
encyclopedia of ancient Greece and Rome, 1st vol. 1. Oxford:
Oxford University
Press

Gantz, Timothy (1993). Early Greek myth. A guide to literary
and artistic sources, 2 vols. Baltimore & London: The Johns
Hopkins University
Press

García Sanjuán, Leonardo. In: Simon, Raúl. Una investigación
bucea hasta el Neolítico para encontrar los orígines de la
desigualdad entre hombres y mujeres. In: El País 15.04.2021

Gimbutas, Marija (1991). The civilization of the goddess. The
world of Old Europe. San Francisco: HarperCollins
- (1996). Die Zivilisation der Göttin. Die Welt des Alten
Europa. Frankfurt am Main: Zweitausendeins

Greene, Ellen (ed.) (1996). Reading Sappho. Contemporary
approaches.
Berkeley, Los Angeles & London: University of California
Press

Groll, Tina: Anfangs hat man uns kein halbes Jahr gegeben.
zeit-online,
22.11.2019

Guérot, Ulrike (2016). Warum Europa eine Republik werden
muss! Eine politische Utopie. Bonn: J.H.W. Dietz

Gurny, Ruth / Ringger, Beat / Seifert, Kurt / Stocker, Monika (2018).
Gutes Alter. Zürich: Pro-Senectute-Bibliothek

Haarmann, Harald (1996). Die Madonna und ihre griechischen Töchter.
Rekonstruktion einer kulturhistorischen Genealogie.
Hildesheim, Zürich
& New York: Olms

- (2006) Sprachenschutz und Kulturerhaltung als
  Menschenpflicht - Bausteine sprachsoziologischer Forschung
  im Informationszeitalter, in:
Sociolinguistica 20: 57-69

- (2010). Einführung in die Donauschrift. Hamburg: Buske

- (2011a). Das Rätsel der Donauzivilisation. Die Entdeckung
  der ältesten Hochkultur Europas. München: C.H. Beck (4th
  edition of 2021)

- (2011b). Writing as technology and cultural ecology.
  Explorations of the human mind at the dawn of history.
  Frankfurt, Bern, Berlin, Oxford
& New York: Peter Lang

- (2012). Indo-Europeanization - day one. Elite recruitment and
  the beginnings of language politics. Wiesbaden: Harrassowitz

- (2013). Mythos Demokratie - Antike Herrschaftsmodelle im
  Spannungsfeld von Egalitätsprinzip und Eliteprinzip.
  Frankfurt, Berlin, Oxford & New York: Peter Lang

- (2014). Roots of ancient Greek civilisation. The influence of
  Old Europe. Jefferson, North Carolina: McFarland

- (2016). Auf den Spuren der Indoeuropäer. Von den
  neolithischen Steppennomaden bis zu den frühen
  Hochkulturen. Munich: C.H. Beck

- (2017). Plato's ideal of the Common Good. Anatomy of a concept of timeless significance. Frankfurt, Berlin, Oxford & New York: Peter Lang

- (2018). Who taught the ancient Greeks the craft of shipbuilding? On the pre-Greek roots of maritime technological know-how, in: Mankind Quarterly 59/2: 155-170

- (2018). Die Verwandlung der Sophia - Vom Ausklang der Aufklärung ins performative Zeitalter. Erster Teil: Auf den Spuren des verlorenen ganzheitlichen Denkens - Das Korrektiv zum Illusionspotenzial der Aufklärung mit ihrem Vernunftsmonopol, ihrer Geschichtsmythologie und ihren Zukunftsvisionen. Berlin: LIT Verlag

- (2019). Plato's sophia. His philosophical endeavor in light of its spiritual currents and undercurrents. Amherst, New York: Cambria

- (2020). Advancement in ancient civilizations. Life, culture, science and thought. Jefferson, North Carolina: McFarland

Haarmann, Harald / LaBGC: Von wegen dunkel! in: Frankfurter Rundschau 10. 07. 2018

Haarmann, Harald / LaBGC: Utopie einer idealen Gemeinschaft in: Frankfurter Rundschau 20. 01. 2019

Hall, Jonathan M. (2002). Hellenicity between ethnicity and culture. Chicago & London: The University of Chicago Press

Hall, Edith (2014). Introducing the ancient Greeks. From Bronze Age seafarers to navigators of the western mind. New York & London: Norton

Haas, Randal (2020): Female hunters of early Americas in: Science Advances, Vol. 6, No. 45

Held, David (2006). Models of democracy. Cambridge &
Malden, MA:
polity (3rd ed.)

Hessel, Stéphane (2011). Empört euch! München: Ullstein

Hinrichs, Uwe (2018). Die Verwandlung der Sophia - Vom
Ausklang der
Aufklärung ins performative Zeitalter. Zweiter Teil: Die
Erzeugung der
Welt. Ein Schritt ins performative Zeitalter. Berlin: LIT Verlag

Hodder, Ian (2004). Women and men at Çatalhöyük, in:
Scientific
American (January 2004): 76-83

- (2006). Çatalhöyük - The leopard´s tale. Revealing the
mysteries of
Turkey´s ancient 'town'. London: Themes & Hudson

Ilievski, Petar Chr. (2000). Zivotot na mikencite vo nivnite
pismeni svedostva, so poseben osvrt kon onomastickite i
prosopografski izvodi (The life of the Mycenaeans from their
own records, with special regard to the onomastic and
prosopographic deductions).

Skopje: Makedonska Akademija na naukite i umetnostite
Isager, Signe / Skydsgaard, Jens Erik (1995). Ancient Greek
agriculture.
An introduction. London & New York: Routledge

Jones, Nicholas (2004). Rural Athens under the democracy.
Philadelphia: University of Pennsylvania Press

Kaulbach, Friedrich (1988). Immanuel Kants „Grundlegung zur
Metaphysik der Sitten". Interpretation und Kommentar.
Darmstadt: Wissenschaftliche Buchgesellschaft

Kazdová, Eliska / Podborsky, Vladimír (eds.) (2007). Studium
sociálních a duchovních struktur praveku - Studium der
sozialen und geistlichen Strukturen der Urzeit. Brno: FF MU

Kirsten, E. (1956). Die griechische Polis als historisch-
geographisches
Problem des Mittelmeerraumes. Bonn: Colloquium
Geographicum 5

Kloss, Heinz (1969). Grundfragen der Ethnopolitik im 20.
Jahrhundert.
Vienna and Stuttgart: Wilhelm Braumüller

Knight, Chris (2011). Early human kinship was matrilineal, in:
Allen et al. 2011: 61-82

Kondylis, Panajotis (1987). Marx und die griechische Antike -
Zwei
Studien. Heidelberg: Manutius Verlag

Kozlarek, O. / Rüsen, J. / Wolff, E. (2012a). Introduction -
Towards a humane world of many worlds, in: Kozlarek et al.
2012b: 9-22

Kozlarek, O. / Rüsen, J. / Wolff, E. (eds.) (2012b). Shaping a
humane world. Civilizations - Axial times - modernities -
humanisms. Bielefeld:
Transcript Verlag

Kristiansen, Kristian (1998). Europe before history. Cambridge
& New
York: Cambridge University Press

Kröner, Hans-Otto (1997). Marcus Tullius Cicero, in: Schütze
1997:
166-173

Kuhn, Steven L. in: Miguel Àngel Criado. La cazadora que
reescribió la prehistoria in: El País, 14. 11. 2020

Kuhn, Steven L. / Stiner, Mary C. (2006). What's a Mother to
Do? The Division of Labor among Neandertals and Modern
Humans in Eurasia.
Current Anthropology Volume 47, No. 6

LaBGC / Haarmann, Harald (2019). MITEINANDER NEU-DENKEN.
Europa im Gestern | Alteuropa im Heute. Berlin: LIT Verlag

LaBGC / Haarmann, Harald (2021). Re-Thinking togetherness.
Know. Act. Now. (englische Übersetzung von LaBGC &
Haarmann 2019, mit einem Nachwort von Harald Seubert).
Berlin: LIT Verlag

Laffineur, Robert (2010). Thorikos, in: Cline 2010: 712-721

Lang, Mabel (2004). The Athenian citizen. Democracy in the
Athenian
Agora. Athen: American School of Classical Studies at Athens
(2. ed.)

Lape, Susan (2010). Race and citizen identity in the classical
Athenian democracy. Cambridge and New York: Cambridge
University Press

Lazarovici, Cornelia-Magda (2009). Cucuteni ceramics:
technology, typology, evolution, and aesthetics, in: Anthony /
Chi 2009: 128-161

Lazarovici, Gheorghe / Drasovean, Florin / Maxim, Zoia
(2001). Parța,
2 volumes Timisoara: Editura Waldpress

Lévêque, P. (1996). The *da-root. Repartition and democracy,
in: Curtis
1996: 128-133

Lütge, Christoph (2007). Was hält eine Gesellschaft
zusammen? Ethik im Zeitalter der Globalisierung. Tübingen:
Mohr Siebeck

Lutz, Mark J. (2012). Divine law and political philosophy in
Plato´s
Laws. DeKalb, IL: Northern Illinois University Press

Maisels, Charles Keith (1999). Early civilizations of the Old World. The formative histories of Egypt, the Levant, Mesopotamia, India and China. London & New York: Routledge

Malkin, Irad (2011). A small Greek world. Networks in the ancient Mediterranean. Oxford & New York: Oxford University Press

Mallory, J.P./Adams, D.Q. (eds.) (1997). Encyclopedia of Indo-European culture. London & Chicago: Fitzroy Dearborn Publishers

Marler, Joan (2006). The myth of universal patriarchy, in: Feminist Theology 14: 163-187

Martin, R.P. (1989). The language of heroes: Speech and performance in the *Iliad*. Ithaca & London

Martin, Thomas R. / Smith, Neel / Stuart, Jennifer F. (2003). Democracy in the *Politics* of Aristotle, in: Blackwell 2003

McInerney, Jeremy (2000). The folds of the Parnassos: Land and ethnicity in ancient Phokis. Austin: University of Texas Press

Meier, Christian (1995). Athen. Ein Neubeginn der Weltgeschichte. Munich: Goldmann

Meyer, Peter (2004). Social evolution, in: Wuketits / Antweiler 2004: 121-169

Mikalson, Jon D. (1991). Honor thy gods. Popular religion in Greek tragedy. Chapel Hill & London: University of North Carolina Press

Missiou, Anna (2011). Literacy and democracy in fifth-century Athens. Cambridge and New York: Cambridge University Press

Mitchell, Lynette G. / Rhodes, P.J. (eds.) (1997). The development of the polis in archaic Greece.London & New York: Routledge

Mittnik, Alissa et. al. Kinship-based social inequality in Bronze Age Europe. In: Sience 10. 10. 2019

Mount, Ferdinand (2010). Full circle. How the classical world came
back to us. London & New York: A CBS Company

Müller, Klaus E. (1987). Das magische Universum der Identität. Elementarformen sozialen Verhaltens - Ein ethnologischer Grundriss.
Frankfurt & New York: Campus

Musti, D. / Sacconi, A. / Rocchetti, L. (eds.) (1991). La transizione dal miceneo all'alto arcaismo: Dal palazzo alla città. Atti del Convegno Internazionale, Rome, 14-19 March 1988. Rome: Consiglio Nazionale delle Ricerche

Nilsson, Martin Persson (1967). Geschichte der griechischen Religion, volume 1: Die Religion Griechenlands bis auf die griechische Weltherrschaft. Munich: C.H. Beck (3rd ed.)

Ober, Josiah (2008). Democracy and knowledge. Innovation and learning in classical Athens. Princeton, NJ & Oxford: Princeton University
Press

Osborne, Robin (1985). Demos, the discovery of classical Attika. Cambridge & New York: Cambridge University Press
- (1996). Greece in the making, 1200 - 479 B.C. New York: Routledge

Parker, Robert (1986). Greek religion, in: Boardman et al. 1986: 248-
268

Popper, Karl Raimund (1957). Die offene Gesellschaft und ihre Feinde, volume 1: Der Zauber Platons. Tübingen: Mohr Siebeck

Pritchett, W.K. (1953). The Attic stelai, part 1, in: Hesperia 22: 225-299

- (1956). The Attic stelai, part 2, in: Hesperia 25: 178-317

Reinhard, Kenneth (2012). Introduction. Badiou's sublime translation of the *Republic*, in: Badiou 2012: vii-xxiii

Roberts, Jennifer T. (1994). Athens on trial. The antidemocratic tradition in western thought. Princeton, NJ: Princeton University Press

Roberts, Mary Nooter / Roberts, Allen F. (1996). Memory - Luba art and the making of history. New York: The Museum for African Art;
Munich: Prestel

Robinson, Eric W. (1997). The first democracies. Early popular government outside Athens. Stuttgart: Franz Steiner Verlag

Rönne, Ronja von (2017). Heute ist leider schlecht (collected columns). Frankfurt: Fischer

Roselli, David Kawalko (2011). Theater of the people. Spectators and society in ancient Athens. Austin: University of Texas Press

Schmidt, Helmut (eds.) (1997). Allgemeine Erklärung der Menschenpflichten - Ein Vorschlag. München & Zürich: Piper

Schmitt, Tassilo (2010). Der Damos von Pylos. Neue Überlegungen zur politischen und sozialen Struktur in der mykenischen Zeit, in: Dement'eva / Schmitt 2010: 9-22

Schütze, Oliver (eds.) (1997). Metzler Lexikon antiker Autoren. Stuttgart & Weimar: J.B. Metzler

Schwinn, Thomas (2001). Differenzierung ohne Gesellschaft. Umstellung eines soziologischen Konzepts. Weilerswist: Velbrück Wissenschaft

Seubert, Harald (2017). Platon - Anfang, Mitte und Ziel der Philosophie.
Freiburg: Karl Alber

- (2019). Panik als Signal praktischer Vernunft. in: Frankfurter Rundschau, 29. 03. 2019

Simpson, Peter L. (1998). A philosophical commentary on the *Politics* of Aristotle. Chapel Hill: University of North Carolina Press

Spikins, Penny (2008). Mesolithic Europe: Glimpses of another world, in: Bailey / Spikins 2008: 1-17

Stanton, G.R. (1990). Athenian politics c 800 - 500 BC: A sourcebook.
London: Routledge

Staune, Jean (2019). L'intelligence collective - Clé du monde de demain. Paris: Éditions de l'Observatoire

Stoneman, Richard (2011). The ancient oracles - Making the gods speak. New Haven & London: Yale University Press

Stucke, Angelika (2012). Leben im roten Utopia. In: Spiegel online, 30.
04. 2012

Thomas, Rosalind (1992). Literacy and orality in ancient Greece.
Cambridge: Cambridge University Press

Tiersch, Claudia (2010). Politische Vorteile durch adlige Vorfahren? Aristokraten in der athenischen Demokratie (5./4. Jh. v. Chr.), in: Dement'eva / Schmitt 2010: 77-92

Trankovits, Laszlo (2011). Weniger Demokratie wagen. Wie Wirtschaft und Politik wieder handlungsfähig werden.
Frankfurt: F.A.Z.-Institut für Management-, Markt- und Medieninformationen

Trojanow, Ilja (2018). Ein Dorf macht sein Ding. In: Die Zeit,

14.11.2018

Tzshoppe, Petra (2016). Mit weiblichem Applaus als Belohnung... – Geschlecht und Teilhabe im olympischen Sport. In: Bildungspotenziale der Olympischen Idee, Baden-Baden: Akademia Verlag

Waterfield, Robin (2009). Why Socrates died: Dispelling the myths.
London: Faber and Faber
Wilson, John-Paul (1997). The nature of overseas settlements in the archaic period: emporion or apoikia? in: Mitchell / Rhodes 1997: 199-207

Wuketits, Franz M. / Antweiler, Christoph (eds.) (2004). Handbook of
evolution, vol. 1: The evolution of human societies and cultures. Weinheim: WILEY-VCH Verlag

Wüst, F.R. (1954-55). Amphiktyonie, Eidgenossenschaft, Symmachie, in: Historia 3: 129-153

Young, Michael (1958). The rise of the meritocracy, 1870-2033. An essay on education and inequality. London: Thames & Hudson

Illustrations

Illustration 1: The heartland of Old Europe and the interconnection of the economic area: routes of domestic trade and external contacts

Illustration 2: The "condominium" ofParța, Banat (see Lazarovici et al. 2001: 257)

Illustration 3: The division of tribes in the Athenian state: model of the

monuments of the naming heroes (see Lang 2004: 9)

Illustration 4: The oldest cadastral register in Europe with information on municipal land ownership (linear text B from Pylos; PY Ep 301)

Illustration 5: model of the theatre of Thorikos (see Roselli 2011: 69)

Illustration 6: Conceptualization and categorization of forms of domination in the work *Politika* by Aristotle (see Book III, chap. 7-14; book IV, chapter 4-10)

Harald Haarmann, a German linguist and cultural philosopher and resident of Finnland; Vice President of the Institute of Archaeomythology and Director of its European Branch; his research has for many years focused on Old Europe as the cradle of the basic values of the Western civilization.

LaBGC, an artist and publicist living in Spain; she is interested in egalitarian forms of society with a peaceful orientation, which motivated her to collaborate with Harald Haarmann; together they have written several books in German and English.

Bibliographic Information of the German National Library. The German National Library registers this publication in the German National Bibliography; detailed bibliographic data on the Internet at http://d-nb.de.

Layout, cover and typesetting: Kristina Schippling
Cover photo – LaBGC 2014_Hallazgo 5_Fund 5 230x100
(nach Grundriss Cucuteni-Siedlung, Ukraine)

ISBN: 978-3-98795-020-9

Printed in Poland
by Amazon Fulfillment
Poland Sp. z o.o., Wrocław
13 August 2023

c95c77bc-fc1a-4375-b23c-4eb526fdec2fR01